Worrier to Warrior

a mother's journey
from fear to faith

Mimika Cooney

Invitation

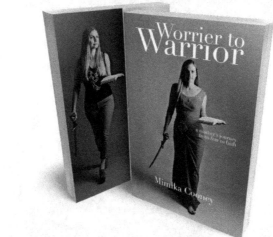

Copyright

Worrier to Warrior: A Mother's Journey from Fear to Faith. First Edition. Copyright © Mimika Cooney 2018.

ISBN 978-1-7322848-1-4 (eBook)
ISBN 978-1-7322848-0-7 (Paperback)
ISBN 978-1-7322848-2-1 (Hardcover)
ISBN 978-1-7322848-3-8 (Audiobook)

Cover Photo: Copyright © Mimika Cooney, Michael Cooney. Cover Design (back and front): Mimika Cooney

Unless otherwise indicated, all Scripture quotations are taken from the Holy Bible, New International Version®, NIV®. Copyright ©1973, 1978, 1984, 2011 by Biblica, Inc.™. The "NIV" and "New International Version" are trademarks registered in the United States Patent and Trademark Office by Biblica, Inc.™

The people and events described and depicted in this book are for educational purposes only. While every attempt has been made to verify information provided in this book, the author assumes no responsibility for any errors, inaccuracies or omissions. If advice concerning medical matters is needed, the services of a qualified professional should be sought. This book is not intended for use as a source of medical advice. The examples within the book are not intended to represent or guarantee that anyone will achieve their desired results. Each individuals success will be determined by his or her desire, dedication, effort and motivation. There are no guarantees you will achieve the desired outcome; the tools, stories and information are provided as examples only.

Please note that Mimika Cooney has made the stylistic choice to capitalize certain words and pronouns that refer to the Father, Son, Holy Spirit, Christ, although it may differ from the stylistic choices of other publishers. For spelling purposes the use of British English is used throughout.

This book and all other materials is published by Mimika Cooney. If you would like more information on Mimika Cooney and her ministry, or would like to purchase more materials, please visit www.MimikaCooney.com

Worrier to Warrior

Worrier to Warrior

A Mother's Journey from Fear to Faith

MIMIKA COONEY

MIMIKA COONEY
CHARLOTTE, NORTH CAROLINA, USA.

Dedication

Dedication

This book is dedicated to my wonderful husband, Michael, my three beautiful children, my mother, my sister and close friends and family who have journeyed with me throughout this process. I could not have done this without your prayer support, encouragement and love. You have taught me what true love is and you have made my life richer by showing unconditional love, support and patience.

I thank my Lord Jesus Christ for putting His covering on me at a young age and for carrying me through each season and storm in my life. Thank you for your patience and your constant whispers of encouragement to "just keep going" so that I wouldn't give up on the dreams you birthed in my heart. I now know that every pain has had a purpose. Looking back on the tapestry of my life, I see Your hand has created something beautiful. I am humbled and honoured that you have chosen me to share my story for Your glory.

This book is in honour of my mother-in-law, Heide, who taught me about inner healing at age 16; and loved me through the years as her own daughter. I am sure she is looking down from heaven with pride.

I also dedicate this book to every mother, grand mother, daughter, sister, aunt, and woman who has ever felt rejected, unlovable, misunderstood, unworthy, or broken. My darling you ARE loved so so much by God! I'm honored to be your host as we reveal God's perfect love and blessings for you life as we uncover His divine plan in this book.

Contents

Foreward

What I share in the following pages is my own personal story of how God revealed himself to me in a very personal way. The Holy Spirit has taught me through the fires, trials and testings about God's eternal love and promise He has for all of His children.

I came to know Jesus at the tender age of 10 years old, and throughout my life I can see the bread crumbs God left along the path to guide me to His heart. Often times my misguided understanding and immaturity would veer me off the path in pursuit of my selfish ambitions, yet God was with me every step of the way guiding me home.

This is a love letter from one mother to another. I know you, I see you, I feel your pain. I know that God sees you too. Everything I share is from walking through it myself. Every lesson I have had to learn the hard way with God's guidance. What I have learnt is that God is the ultimate heart surgeon.

For twenty years I have been an entrepreneur and creative, and along the way God hijacked my heart and my goals, and opened my eyes to what truly matters in life. I pray that God reveals himself to you and imparts to your heart the knowledge of His Word, and you have assurance of His love for your own life. My goal is to share this portion of my life and let you decide what it means for you.

With love
Mimika

1. My Story

The Catalyst

It was February in Florida. I had just finished a full day at a conference and I received a call from my husband. I had a feeling that something was up but I just couldn't put my finger on it. During the conversation I asked how our kids were doing and he explained that we had a big problem. One of our children had spiraled into a very dark place. I knew the situation had come to a head where we had to deal with it immediately. The situation had been boiling for the past five years and now it was undeniably affecting everyone. Having to endure two more days at the conference before returning home were excruciatingly painful. Those two days were a blur.

My beautiful child with bright blue eyes, a charming smile and kind heart had a broken spirit. This is one of the most devastating and heartbreaking things a parent can witness happening to a child and it broke my heart. Fear gripped my heart. Every time I thought about the situation my chest would tighten, my stomach would clench and I felt nauseous. My heart raced like I was running a marathon and my hands would shake, even at rest. I lived on adrenaline. My mind would imagine every horror ending, and I felt totally out of control. Anything I knew to fix the problem I tried but to no avail.

Things spiraled down, my business fell apart and I had what some would call an identity crisis. In the previous years we had immigrated from South Africa to England, and again from England to the USA within a 5 year period. I had birthed two babies and started a business all within those 5 years. I had built a successful photography business, won professional photography awards and had garnered a good name in the photography industry. I had written two books on the subject, and I was invited to speak at professional conventions in the UK and USA. Then the

2008 crash happened. The ripple affected my high end portrait business and it ground to a halt. Clients dried up and I was left exhausted, disappointed and without a purpose. I tried three online business launches and they all failed. The pressure, guilt and disappointments were rising as I racked up $11,000 of credit card debt that I kept secret from my husband. All through my life when people told me I was too young or incapable of doing something, I was determined to prove them wrong. When someone said I couldn't achieve it, it was a big motivator for me and I would say to myself "I'll show you!". I had developed a bad attitude and it tainted everything.

Less than three months later our family was delivered a heavy blow when my beloved mother-in-law passed away after battling cancer for two hard years. My faith was rocked! I had so many questions. How could God allow this to happen? Why weren't our prayers answered? Why did He let her suffer so much? She had lived her life on fire for Jesus and yet she had experienced such excruciating pain, endured debilitating chemo and radiation; and her last year of life was spent confined to a wheelchair.

After her passing I experienced physical grief like I had never experienced before. My body was exhausted, I couldn't talk without heave crying (you know the ugly kind of snot crying). I felt nauseous for weeks and I lost all desire to do anything that brought me joy. I hadn't seen her since our last visit to South Africa two years earlier, and what broke my heart was that I hadn't had the chance to say goodbye. I kept asking "Why does God allow bad things to happen to good people?" and I questioned why God was not answering me.

I couldn't deal with the clutter in my home, my self-inflicted to-do list felt suffocating, I lost my passion. I was in denial. I had exhausted everything I could do in my own strength, and now I had to put my faith in action and stand on His Word that God would make a way. As a recovering perfectionist and control freak, it was hard for me to just do like Elsa and "Let it go!". I cried out to God "Lord please help me, show me what to do to fix the situation".

Everything I had believed before, I now questioned. I felt like Isaiah 64:6 "all our deeds of righteousness are like filthy rags", as the things I had previously valued now seemed meaningless. My faith floundered and I felt forsaken. I lived in my pajamas and I couldn't get off the couch. I couldn't bring myself to admit it, but I was depressed. My mind became the battlefield. The enemy bombarded me with lies and discouragement, and I constantly questioned my self worth. It felt like the season I was in was what some call the dark night of the soul. It felt like it would never end, yet I knew God was up to something. All I could do to keep from drowning was to focus on Hebrews 12:2 "fixing our eyes on Jesus, the pioneer and perfecter of faith".

As I prayed for healing, God was doing a deep work in me. Once I decided to stop pretending that everything was fine, and was willing to admit to myself, my family and God that we had a problem; only then could God start the heart healing process within me.

Then I remembered the dream.

December 17th 2010 I awoke in the middle of the night sobbing uncontrollably that my husband woke me up in a panic. I was crying out loud "No! No! No!". As a child I had experienced nightmares, but this was so vivid and so real I was physically crying out aloud and thrashing about. The scene was idyllic. Green grass, mountain views and a fresh breeze. A house embedded on a hill overlooking a flowing stream. I'm at the house to pick up my child from hanging out with friends, and I'm searching every room. The group of friends are enjoying a game of pool, and as I enter the room they stop and stare at me. They don't respond but look at me surprised and I get the feeling that they are not telling me something.

I start to panic and run through the house gaining speed yelling loudly but I get no answer. I burst through the sliding doors into the back garden and I spot the stream with large overhanging willow trees. Immediately my instincts told me to cross the river. The water that appeared from a distance to be a shallow stream, started to pick up speed. As I approached the waters edge I jumped into the water. The swells became more violent and I eventually made it to the other side after much effort as my husband followed close behind me. Then I spotted something floating on the river bed behind a broken tree. I rushed over to it and discovered a body that lay face down in the river wrapped in plastic wrap. I frantically grabbed the body and turned it over. I noticed the hands stuck in a surrendered position, and those big blue eyes were wide open and glazed over. He looked dead. I screamed loudly "No! No! No!" as I frantically ripped the plastic wrap off. My husband and I dragged the body out of the water onto the ground. The last thing I remembered was the panic of us trying to revive him, when I heard my husband's audible voice say, "it's okay, it's okay relax it's only a dream". I awoke to find my voice box feeling raw and the realization that I had a dream. To this day I will never forget how real it felt.

Seven years later the meaning of that dream had finally become clear. God had given me a warning of things to come, but instead of seeking Him for the answers, I allowed myself to ignore the warning and deny it was happening. I've since learnt not to disregard my dreams and seek God first before I need to learn things the hard way.

The Revelation

My husband and I grew up in South Africa and the way we were taught to deal with things was you either "do it or else." We grew up with a healthy respect for authority, and knew that there was no time for being a "sissie" (South African for being weak or soft). There was always the threat of punishment and you respected what your elders said, so you just learnt to comply (whether you felt like it or not). It didn't matter how you felt, you just kept going, you got back up and did it again. Perhaps it was due to my classical ballet training from the age of three by a strict teacher who expected nothing but the best, and constant repetition to get things right. My memories of being in school were feelings of frustration and confinement. We spent most of our time playing outdoors doing some sort of sport or activity, so if you were not into sports you were severely marginalized, labeled and teased for not fitting in.

The kind of personality I have is if there is something wrong, you look at the root cause and fix it. We followed the 'typical' parenting advice. We confiscated the cell phone, electronics and computer when the rules were broken. Our child was not responding to the typical" parenting discipline and advice that everyone (family included) were telling us to do. The judgement and criticism was heart wrenching. The shame had set in and we didn't want others to know what the situation was really like, so we shut ourselves away and withdrew from socializing. It was easier to keep to ourselves than to open up our home to others who may look down on us for failing as parents. Soon the fear overtook me. The fear was debilitating enough for me to stop what I was doing and force me to focus on the problem.

The reality is that we are living in the 21st century. Clearly an old school method and approach to raising children in an environment that has changed just doesn't work. We are raising kids with so much more stimulus, technology, and information at their fingertips it had become information overload. Their brains have to contain so much more information, expectation, and knowledge, that they don't know how to process it all. The hard "just do it" approach clearly wasn't working in our household. The parenting books needed to be burnt and Dr. Spock had to go!

To admit that my knees had calluses from all the praying I did is an understatement. Not knowing what to do next with my limited knowledge, experience and strength; I felt hopeless as a parent. I cried so much it hurt to breathe. I felt like an utter failure as a mother, a wife and a woman. I was hard on myself. I thought "I'm a business owner. I've achieved all these accolades. I've been able to organize two immigration's to two countries, and here I am, I can't even keep it together in my own home!" As adults we continue using the same methods because they have become a habit. We forget that when we were kids, we sometimes felt like we could not cope so we ran to

Mommy to make things better. But now we are grown up, we don't want to ask for help.

It took others looking in to the situation to point out that I needed to deal with what was going on within me before I could help anyone else. Thank heavens for mothers and sisters who love us enough to tell us the truth, even though we may not want to hear it! I started to do some internal work and realized I couldn't continue to try to cope with what was going on, I was a hot mess. Denial was no longer an option. Everything I thought I knew was being challenged, everything from my parenting skills to my faith.

Throughout my life, I've always had a heart for praying and following what God wanted me to do. Growing up in a tense environment, coupled with circumstances I couldn't control (like my parents divorce), had caused me to become a fixer. I always needed to fix the problems. Being strategy minded and very determined not to give in or give up, I was adamant I would find a way to fix things. My natural default is to rely on myself. I admit it, I'm a recovering perfectionist and control freak! I suspect it goes back to my lack of trust. Okay, I admit it too I have trust issues, but more on that later...

What I had realized is that I had spent so much time seeking answers from man, that I forgot to ask the one person who had all the answers in the world – God. Once I had come to the end of my rope and discovered I couldn't rely on myself anymore (or anyone else) I finally found Him. My only regret is that I didn't look for God earlier, because He was there the whole time. Finally, during a morning prayer time I had the revelation. I realized deep roots of rejection, pride, fear, resentment, and judgment (to name a few) that had been planted in my early years was holding me back. They had developed into trees of habit, and mindsets that had developed rotten fruit.

This book is a journey of how I came to realize that God is the ultimate heart surgeon. Once I relented to His will He was able to heal my hurts and fears and completely renew my mind.

The Early Years

Growing up on a twelve acre farm in South Africa in the 80's was my everyday norm. I remember how it felt to walk shoeless on the kakiebos grass looking for my next adventure with my dog, Kelly, following close behind me. We had our own horses (that I enjoyed riding), donkeys, rabbits, a vegetable garden, and a pond filled with carp fish. My entrepreneurial father had his own construction business named after me, and for as long as I could remember there was constant traffic of people, tractors and building equipment.

My Yiayia and Papou (Greek grandparents) lived right next door. There was a door that attached their house to ours. Every afternoon I would spend with my Yiayia and she would teach me to cook yummy Greek food, bake delicious treats and help me with my Greek homework. My Papou was the family MacGyver. If there was something broken, Papou was the one to fix it. He had a garage at the back of the house that would house all his tools, gadgets, scrap metal, motor parts, welding machine and all kinds of thingamabobs. My curiosity would get the better of me and often I would sneak in to watch what he was doing only to hear him say 'Mika! Papoocha!" (translated Mika Shoes!) I wasn't fond of wearing shoes, except the ballet slipper kind. My evening performances were the family entertainment. Our lounge coffee table was my stage and I would perform ballet, jazz and flamenco dances to the Beatles, Lionel Richie, and the Gypsy Kings accompanied by the old style record player.

I have fond memories of planting carrots, potatoes and tomatoes in our back garden with Papou. He had a blue tractor he would use to till the soil. He would let me sit on his lap and drive. For my birthday parties he would hitch a trailer to the back of the tractor and the kids would love to ride around the farm. We had castle gates built at the entrance of our dirt road and all the kids thought I lived in a castle. I loved frolicking along the dirt paths, feeling the fresh African wind in my hair and the smell of the red earth in my toes. Some of my best childhood memories were when we enjoyed many wonderful holidays at the beach in Knysna, learning to fish with my Dad on his boat, camping in the caravan, and snorkeling in Greece. I have many fond memories of combined family holidays with my best friend and her family. There was also noise, bustle, kids playing and braais (South African barbecue).

As a baby I was baptized in the Greek Orthodox church, and my Yiayia would take me to church every Easter. We would make the red Easter eggs and a huge feast days before Easter Friday when the entire family would come over. My mouth would water waiting for all the Greek treats we would eat, but only after the church service at midnight (which I could barely stay awake for). Our family get togethers were like a scene out of the movie "My Big Fat Greek Wedding". My Yiayia would teach me to do the cross of the saints, and my mother would say prayers with me each night before bedtime.

I remember the exact moment I lost my childhood wonder. I was ten years old standing by the tennis courts, wearing my ballet leotard and rainbow skirt. My mother turned to me and said; "I don't know what to do, but I have to do what's right for you children". I turned to her and said with great maturity' "You need to do what you think is best mommy." She told me to run to the house and grab a dustbin bag to fill it with as much of my toys and clothes that I could. In a state of panic, we grabbed what we could and threw the bags into the car. We left in a hurry. As we pulled out the driveway, the office secretary ran toward the car, held up our dog and said "Take the dog or he will kill it!". I took one last glimpse through the rear window at the house we called home, knowing that things would never be the same again.

It never felt like a home a child could play freely or relax. It was like a train station of people, equipment and a constant stream of strangers in and out the front door. Running a construction business from home was not conducive to enjoyable family life. Most dinners were interrupted by somebody knocking on the door needing something urgent that required immediate attention, and it often felt like we lived in a train station. The constant fighting and arguing between my parents, and the volatile temper flares often left my sister and I in a state of anxiety. The foreboding sense of fear of what would happen next meant everyday felt like we were walking on eggshells. My sister was about five years old when she had the audacity to ask for more tomato sauce (ketchup) with her dinner. After nagging incessantly, in a fury Dad grabbed the bottle and squeezed it all over her head. We sat in awkward silence for the remainder of the meal with the tomato sauce dripping down my sisters temple that she dared not touch. We were on tender hooks we expected him to fly into a rage as we sat frozen and waited for the ordeal to be over. As a seven-year-old child it was hard to understand why my Dad was always so angry. I would ask myself "Was it my fault? Was I being a bad girl? Is it something I did? Maybe I'm not being good enough."

I remember waking up one night after midnight to hear mom sobbing in the bathtub. I went to ask her what was wrong, her eyes red and puffy, and through the tears she told me to go back to bed and said everything would be fine. Even though I was ten years old, I felt like I had the weight of the world on my shoulders. I do not know why I took on the responsibility, perhaps it was because I'm the oldest in the family, but I had this sense that I had to keep it together and be strong for everyone else.

Growing up in South Africa under the restricting apartheid system became a way of life. We had a maid called Mary who loved us like her own. She lived in a room attached to the garage, she cooked for us and cleaned the house while my parents worked in the business right next-door. By living with us she had to live away from her own family. Her children were being raised by her mother in the rural hills of her hometown. It never occurred to me what a sacrifice she had to make to help care for our family. But in the 1980's South Africa it was the way of life for a domestic to earn an income for their family. I can't imagine the pain she must have felt being stripped of her right to be a mother and raise her own children. Even though as kids we were not fully aware of what apartheid really meant, we were aware that there was some kind of separation. It used to bother me the way people would treat the blacks like they were second rate citizens. I had this sense of shame and guilt for being white. We had been given special privileges only because we were born different. I was grateful that I did not have to endure that kind of suffering. Even as a young child I just tried to be nice and treat people with respect to make up for the appalling way they were being treated by those around me.

It was around 3am one Friday night that I awoke to the sound of police sirens at the back of the house. I snuck out of bed to investigate the commotion. I peered through the curtains and saw a police van with its doors wide open, headlights shining bright and the policeman grabbed one of the workers by the collar, punched and yelled profanities at him. He threw the guy into the back of the truck, and started hitting another guy with his police baton, he beat him as he was thrown into the back of the van. The Afrikaans policeman yelled at the other workers, who stood half dressed from being rudely woken up, "Where is your pass?! Where is your pass?!"

At that time in South Africa no black person was permitted to leave their homeland and work in the city without a "pass". My mother's job was to get all the paperwork and "passes" in order whenever they hired someone new. Even though the workers on our property had been properly documented, the police would conduct these surprise raids just to squeeze monetary bribes. After some heated discussion and payment of a fine at the police station, the problem would go away and everyone was free to go. With the frustrations and the restrictions of the apartheid system, my parents had to battle with authorities with legal issues just to have the construction workers arrive for work everyday. The political uncertainty in the country affected everyone. Petrol prices went up regularly and without notice, which would affect the prices of the cost of materials and supplies. The constant theft of building supplies and burglaries on our property caused a security risk; and we lived behind seven foot walls, burglar bars and alarms. This lack of control infuriated my Dad and aggravated an already volatile situation. It felt like we were living on a time bomb ready to explode. When you are dealing with the stress of running a business in a politically unstable country, where a single word from the President can send the prices of petrol, milk and bread skyrocketing; you learned to get used to the uncertainty.

Looking back now as an adult, I understand why my Dad was so stressed, especially about the things he could not control. People deal with frustration, anxiety and stress in different ways and his anger outbursts were probably his way of releasing his frustrations. As a child all I could see was anger, fear and family discord that pervaded our home and there was no peace. Knowing what I know now as a 40-year-old married woman, is that our pride and sense of worth can get tied up in what we do for a living. Along the way circumstances can cause a dream to be left to die. My parents started out as a really good team, but in time something happened. They lost their vision, they lost hope, compromises were made, and things changed. People make different choices based on their own values, and their values started parting ways. Mom decided to proceed with a divorce and became a real estate agent. Dad tried to get his family back together and they tried to reconcile, but it didn't last very long.

Each of us have our own viewpoint of how things transpired in our childhood, and our reality is our reality. Now that I am a parent, I know how hard it is to be perfect in your child's eyes because perfect doesn't exist.

Soon after my parents divorced I attended Rhema Bible church with my grandparents, a mega church in South Africa, and I gave my life to Jesus at the age of ten years old. I was so eager in my new found commitment I said to the Lord "Here am I send me!". I remember clearly hearing the Holy Spirit say "it won't be easy but if you keep your eyes fixed on Jesus I will do great things through you." Little did I know what that declaration would mean for me.

The Rude Awakening

I never felt accepted growing up. I was teased incessantly and was often called "barbarian" because of my surname. Most kids experience some form of teasing as they grow up, but when it starts to affect a child's character and view of the world, that is when it becomes a problem. It seemed like things would never get better for me with the tension at home, and being teased at school. I felt hopeless and very much alone.

I do not remember the exact moment it happened, it was more like a slow chipping away at my self confidence.

Once my parents divorced we moved away and I started at a new school. I hoped that a fresh start at a new school would allow me to make new friends who understood me better. Being the new kid in class was scary and it was hard to fit in amongst kids who had established friendship groups. I just kept quiet and to myself to avoid any confrontation. What surprised me was that I found myself feeling the same rejection once again, and being misunderstood made me retreat more into myself. It was like I had a target on my back and I couldn't understand why.

At thirteen years old I had an experience that left lasting scars for years. It was the end of the school day when the bell rang and all the kids were walking toward the gates for their parents to pick them up. I had learned the knack of weaving through the traffic of people at a hurried pace so I could get to the gate as fast as I could to avoid detection. However, this day proved to be different. As I made my way down the back corridor by the main hallway I found myself cornered by two girls. I realized that I would have to make a run for it if I was going to get out of this pickle. As I picked up speed I pushed past one girl who grabbed my backpack, and in the hurry I dropped it and sprinted to the fence. The other girl cornered me and I had to dart behind the classroom. I was trapped. Before I knew it, both girls were on top of me pushing me against the metal fence, grabbing my hair and slapping my face. It all happened so fast that I barely had time to shout for help while defending myself with my hands to protect my face. Just then I heard a teacher scream "Hey leave her alone!" and both girls ran off out of sight. The teacher came to my rescue to see if I was okay and I picked myself up red faced and said that I was fine. I was in shock. The walk home that day was in stunned silence. I felt hurt, angry and betrayed because one of the girls who attacked me had previously professed to be my friend. We had hung out together, had sleepovers, spent the holiday together. Now I felt like I had no one. The worst part was that not a single person at school took action to rectify the situation. Other kids saw these girls treat me cruelly, their taunting jeers and insults were a common occurrence. Yet they did nothing and some even laughed along with them. It is only when my mother got annoyed with my incessant tears that she stepped in and addressed the issue, only then did things change. She demanded a sit down meeting with the girl and her parents to get to the bottom of it. During their meeting after much denial the girl eventually broke down and admitted to her parents and my mother that she was guilty of bullying me. Only then did she back off and leave me alone, the air between us was as cold as ice. The light within me that had burned so brightly when I was younger was slowly being dimmed. I felt rejected, misunderstood, abused, forgotten and alone. My trust in people was broken. I became cynical and questioned everyone's motives. I lost my joy and gave up on dreaming. Two years later my mother could see how badly the situation at school was affecting me, that she made the hard decision to move us once again to give me a fresh start. I wasn't hopeful.

One Friday evening when I was feeling depressed on the couch watching TV (like I did most weekends), my mother insisted I go to the church youth group. I was not interested in putting myself out there to be rejected once again and I refused to go. After much insistence she dragged me there herself. How embarrassing for a fifteen year old to have her mother escort her to a youth group filled with teenagers! Wearing my new white jeans and turquoise shirt, we arrived late and slipped into the back row trying not to be noticed. That night they were putting on a talent show and we arrived just as these two guys with guitars were on stage in the middle of a song. As we sat down I locked eyes with the guy wearing a maroon shirt and for an awkward moment I couldn't look away. My mother turned to me and said "Isn't he cute?" Ugh no dating advice from my mother! I went red in the face. I said that he looked too old and that shirt he was wearing was just awful. It was an awkward hour watching less than talented youths put on a show, and I was counting the minutes to when we could leave. The talent show finally came to an end and I wanted to bolt out of there as quickly as possible. Just as we were about to exit the door the same two guys (without their guitars) stood in front of us blocking the door. One introduced himself and for about 15 minutes my mother exchanged pleasantries as we stood there awkwardly trying not to look embarrassed at the situation. My mother insisted that I could cook and without holding back, gave them my telephone number and invited them to come over for pizza. Wowza I was being set up by my own mother! Ask any teenager and this would be the height of embarrassment, but I wasn't too offended because I did think the guy wearing the maroon shirt was actually super cute.

I waited for the phone to ring for a whole week and nothing. Eventually I gave up thinking I would hear from him again, then the phone rang. Michael and I talked for over an hour and he boldly invited himself over for pizza the next day, since he was taking up my mothers offer. Our first date was hilarious, instead of pizza I thought I would be adventurous and make fish and cake. It turns out that those are two foods that Michael dislikes the most! He arrived early before I had everything prepared, and during our conversation I accidentally left too much wax paper on the baking tray and that it caught fire! Amazingly he forgave my cooking faux pas and he stuck around.

God knew what I needed when I needed it. Although my mother prayed for a Christian girl friend, God sent me a Godly young man who would show me unconditional love. God's plan was in motion but the enemy is like a roaring lion ready to steal, kill and destroy what the Lord has designed. Eighteen months later I was faced with a huge challenge of my faith, my commitment to Michael and our love story was put to the test.

The Test

I awakened from a startling dream that shook me to my core. I had dreamt that I was lying in my bed when this dark silhouette of a man appeared at my bedroom door blocking the doorway. I couldn't make out his facial features but his shape, mannerisms and outline were unforgettable. I felt this foreboding sense of fear as I lay in my bed unable to move. I couldn't understand what it meant.

Two days later my mother returned from a Christian singles weekend she attended and announced that she had met a man. He had proposed on Friday and she accepted on Sunday. I was shocked. Then she proceeded to tell me that we were moving to Durban (which was 6 hours away). I was devastated to have to leave everything I loved behind. The first time we met him was another shock. As he stepped out of his car I immediately recognized his shape, mannerisms and outline as the figure I had seen in my dream. Fear came rushing in but I dare not say anything to upset the apple cart. I wanted my mother to be happy but she wouldn't see the truth or listen to reason. It felt like a tsunami had just rushed through our lives.

Within a couple of weeks we had packed up the house and we were ready to move. I cried and cried for days arguing with my mom that this did not feel right. She insisted I break it off with Michael and move on. I felt hopeless, powerless and heart broken but I would not give up hope. How could I give up on true love? As we drove away I was crying feeling sick to my stomach. All I could do the entire drive down was sing the song "God will make a way when there seems to be no way". God spoke to my heart very clearly and said "If you trust me, I will turn everything around for your good."

The next week spent in a foreign house with foreign people was a blur. What I distinctly remember though was that God was challenging me with something I had closed my heart to. He was asking me to give my Dad another chance. He was asking me to put my pain and fears aside, and to try to repair the relationship. He assured me that He could make all things new. How could I refuse? I did not want to be stuck in this situation and I know God cares so much for me that He had my best interests at heart. I took the leap of faith knowing that it would be hard, but God would be there every step of the way.

Within a day I got news that I could get a ride back up to Johannesburg for a friends wedding. This was my chance to take that step of faith knowing that God would work out the details. Michael and I were reunited what unspeakable joy! They say absence makes the heart grow fonder, and we knew from that day on that we were meant to be together, we are soul mates. God would honour His Word and His plan but I didn't expect that what would happen next would be so painful.

I reached out to my Dad and asked if I could live with him so I could remain in Johannesburg, finish school and continue the life I had built there. He was so happy for the chance for us to spend time together. I knew though that it would unlock a barrage of drama especially with my mother. She was devastated to hear I wanted to live with my Dad, and she took it as personal rejection. But I just knew that the man she met and quickly married was sent to break up our family and cause havoc. I was worried for my little sister and the influence he would have on her, and I prayed that God would protect them both. I had to trust that all things would work out for good.

I was sixteen when my Dad proceeded with the custody application. His lawyer instructed me not to make contact with my mother during the proceedings and it was brutal. I walked around school with a sickening feeling of fear, nausea and despair. I felt like I was being ripped in two between my parents. The court insisted on interviewing my school headmaster, teachers and church pastor. They wanted to determine if I was mature enough to make my own decision of whom I wanted to live with. It was a major invasion of privacy.

My standard nine (junior year) exams were a blur. The night before the court hearing I tried studying for the exam, only to have fail the test miserably. The school considered my special circumstance and expunged the results from my school record. I was numb. All this time I would cry out to God to heal my heart, repair the relationship with my father, and allow my mother to forgive me for the hurt. God is good and His tender mercies endure forever. I was blessed to be supported by Michael's family and friends that I had made at church. They all prayed for me and my situation.

Once the courts awarded custody to my father, my mother declared that I had "divorced" her. She broke off all contact and disappeared with my sister for nine months without a word about their safety or location. I felt like I had lost my mother and sister, and that they would never understand the situation from my view point. I held onto the promise that God would turn everything around for our good. As a mother I can understand how painful it was for my mother to lose me like that. I had caused her pain and it would take time for the wounds to heal. She was caught up in her own point of view, and when emotions run high it is hard to see a situation from both sides of the fence.

Three years later Michael and I were engaged to be married. At this time my mother had already moved to England with my sister and her husband, and I had not seen them for years. The air was taken out my sail when she said she could not attend my wedding. I lost all joy knowing my own mother would not be around to experience the fun things that go into organizing a wedding.

I went into planner mode, shut off my emotions and steam rolled ahead. I rented the first dress I could find that fit me. I missed out on the joyful event of trying on and buying the dress of my dreams with my mother, sister and best friends watching. My mother-in-law was so supportive and tried to help fill in my mother's shoes, but I refused much help. She wanted to do more but in my stubbornness, I just wanted to do as much of it myself just to get it over with (and partly because I felt it would betray my mother by allowing my mother-in-law to step in her absent shoes). I was awful at admitting I needed help and my pride kept me from accepting help.

It seemed that no matter how hard I tried to make things work, something would always come up to ruin things. The night before our wedding Michael was in hospital with a drip in his arm due to dehydration from a stomach bug. I was devastated at the thought that he may not be able to walk down the aisle, and the outdoor ceremony was being threatened by a heavy storm.

Our ceremony was planned for a hot African Summer's day in mid January. The heavy storm had rolled in overnight and changed our outdoor ceremony plans. We were held up in traffic for over an hour by the heavy storm and yes I was an hour late to my own wedding! My plans for an outdoor ceremony quickly turned awry when the storm washed out the garden gazebo and flower arrangements. Guests were hurried into a makeshift conference room with plastic garden chairs. Michael was still sick that morning with a pounding headache, and during our vows he was swaying from side to side feeling dizzy. I gripped his arm tighthly so he would not fall over. We made it through the day and were happy to walk down the makeshift aisle as husband and wife. We honoured the Lord's marriage covenant in our relationship and married a few months short of my twentieth birthday. What a blessing to marry my childhood sweetheart! The enemy tried his best to mess with our plans just like he always does, but God would have the final say. God will always have the final say and He is true to His word.

Romans 8:28 says;

We know that God is always at work for the good of everyone who loves him. They are the ones God has chosen for his purpose.

Second Chances

When my first child was born, I had this longing to reconnect with my own mother. Differences aside, now that I was a mother, I fully understood that there is no bond like a mother has with her own child. I prayed that God would make a way to heal our relationship and our hearts. God is a God of second chances. He always finds a way to fix what we have broken. God in His faithfulness made a way for my mother and I to reconcile our differences.

When my daughter was three months old we decided to take our first trip as a family overseas to visit my mother and sister in England. My husband was apprehensive about how we would be received, since my mother had blamed him for the split over the custody issue. But even though we had our doubts that the trip would help, I was prepared to take the risk. God was making it very clear to me to walk in forgiveness and reconcile our relationship.

It did not make logical or financial sense to spend on an expensive overseas trip especially when we considered how poorly the South African Rand / Pound exchange rate was at the time. Michael's family voiced their opinions about how they thought we were being foolish since our new Internet business was still in its infancy. But I knew it was something we just had to do.

We arrived in England on a warm Summer's day and were warmly greeted by my mother, her husband and my sister at the train station. What a relief! We were expecting cold shoulders and solemn looks, but they were so happy to see us and to meet the newest addition to our family. Granny was smitten with her granddaughter and any hard feelings from the past melted away. Our weeks trip to England was far more enjoyable than we had expected. God dropped the seed into our hearts and opened our eyes to something we had never thought of before. For the first time my husband and I considered that this could be a place we could live and make our home.

After our week in England we went to visit my Greek grandparents who now lived in Rhodes, Greece. I felt the week we spent with my mother and sister was far too short, so we invited them to Greece to vacation with us. They bought a last minute ticket and joined us for another ten days of mediterranean fun. For the first time in twelve years since the divorce, we were all together as a family with my Yiayia and Papou. What I realized during that trip is that family is thicker than water. No matter the circumstances, no matter the pain, no matter the water under the bridge; family is family. There is no problem big enough that God cannot handle!

Upon our return to South Africa we kept feeling that God was calling us to stretch ourselves out of our comfort zone. I expected that the once fleeting thought of living in England was just a holiday feel good moment, but the seed was being watered. For my daughters first birthday both my mother and sister made the trip from England to South Africa to celebrate and attend the party. The bonds were being repaired and it felt like we were right back to where we used to be, the three musketeers!

Six months later I discovered I was pregnant again and we were elated. God was blessing us with another child with the two year age gap we had wanted. The realization soon hit that if we were seriously considering moving to England, we would have to make the decision fast before I was too far along in my pregnancy to travel. We decided that we needed to take the step of faith that we felt God was calling us to do, and immigrate to England. It meant we would have to act fast to get the ball in motion.

It was a very painful decision to leave our family in South Africa, the business we had started, our friends and our church; but we knew it was God. My mother-in-law had grown very close to my daughter as she had babysat her everyday since she was three weeks old while I worked in our home office. It was heart wrenching to deliver the news that life as our family had known it, was going to change. To outsiders it didn't make any sense! Why leave the comforts you already have for something you have no assurance will work out? Crazy I know, but that is how God works.

Within six weeks we had sold our house, most of our furniture and belongings, and boxed up personal things to be shipped to England. We had to give away our beloved pets, our two Dachshund dogs, as we felt they would not survive the six month quarantine. That last Christmas was bittersweet as we said our farewells to our family and prepared ourselves for the unknown. God in His mercies knows all things, and works everything out for our good when we trust Him. Even though there were no assurances that any of it would work out, I knew without any doubt that God would come through and make things right. It was a huge step of faith and big risk, but when God is directing us He knows the end game. If God is for us who can be against us?

The Realization

The truth of the matter is that we all have a similar story, just set in a different setting. The themes of pain, hurt, rejection, fear, disappointment are all too common for many of us. I am sure for many reading this, you may have experienced situations even worse, but let me say that it is never too late to start again. The difference is that we get to choose whether we remain the victim, or we become the victor of our own stories. We get to choose to follow God and His leading.

There are many adults walking around today with wounded souls with pain from their childhood that has resulted in their arrested emotional development. They have never been able to break free from the bondage of their wounds, and it has held them back their entire life. When someone refuses to admit they have a problem they cannot get the help they need. It is almost as if they wear their pain with pride, as if it should garner pity or attention from others. I know because I have been there!

Let's be honest, no one likes the victim mentality. It is polarizing to people who want to get closer to you but fear they will get sucked into the vortex of negativity and your self loathing. Harsh words I know, but they are necessary. Take it from one friend to another, who has been there I want you to be free, I want you to be whole again, and I know God wants that for you too.

Blaming my failings and failures on everyone else, or myself, did not get me anywhere but send me down a lonely road called self pity. The only person at the pity party was me because it only has room for one! I soon find out that it is only once I came to this realization myself, when I stopped suppressing my feelings, that I found myself truly ready to make a change. Once I stopped blaming others for my wounds, and decided it was time to allow God to make me whole again, only then could I make progress with my own story.

Perhaps you might identity with my story, maybe my story is your story too? At the end of the day it is up to you, how will you choose? If you feel far from God and doubt whether there is hope for you, let me assure you darling that there is.

The Healing

But for you who fear my name, the Son of Righteousness will rise with healing in his wings. And you will go free, leaping with joy like calves let out to pasture.

Malachi 4:10

My husband and I were celebrating our 21st wedding anniversary and I clearly heard the Lord say "you need to go to Elevation Church". The Pastor was preaching a series and on the big screen they showed a story about the director working in video production. As she shared her story my heart leapt and I started to cry because I knew then that God was speaking directly to me! I have been a dancer since I was three years old, and having endured years of rejection, pain, loss and grief; I had given up on things that brought me joy. I knew that day that I needed to serve as a video production volunteer and offer my gifts and talents for His Kingdom. I finally had a way to put my gifts to good use and feel like I had a purpose again.

Being part of the online video production volunteer team at Elevation Church helped me take my eyes off my own problems, and focus on doing God's work by being obedient and serving others. It was a huge lesson in humility as I soon realized that I would be under the leadership of people who were half my age! I had to put my 'leader' badge down, put my pride in my pocket, and be willing to serve with a grateful and humble heart. No one cared about my credentials or accomplishments, we were all there to serve the gospel to those in need. Every weekend I spent under the Word of God, listening attentively to the worship songs and sermons, helped saturate my heart and soul with God's truth. Serving others gave me a sense of purpose and helped me step out from the cloud of despair I had been under.

The words to the worship song "Echo" by Elevation Worship became my battle call as I confessed in song God's promises over my life. When fear was calling and my hope was lost I had to focus on God. I had to decide not to give up.

In Proverbs 13:12 it says *"Hope deferred makes the heart sick, but a longing fulfilled is a tree of life."*

God was bringing me out of the wilderness of hope deferred. Soaking myself in His presence slowly but surely was healing the crevices of my broken heart. God the Father was revealing himself to me as He gently lay me down in green pastures and helped me to rest in His presence. The worship song "Here in the Presence" by Elevation Worship became a soothing promise to me of God's love. It says even though our past might be broken we can still move on. No more running away from our hurt or problems because the Lord has open arms ready to receive us.

Psalm 30:11 had become my faith stand *"You have turned my mourning into joyful dancing. You have taken away my clothes of mourning and clothed me with joy"*. God has turned my mourning, pain and heartache into dancing for His glory. What the enemy planned for evil He has turned into good by bringing back joy into my life. Just like the song "There is a Cloud" by Elevation Worship I believe that it is time to lift our eyes to the Lord and receive the healing rain.

We are standing on The Rock and promises that God has given our family and we are walking it out through faith. We are not meant to do life alone, and it is only when we reach out and become part of the community, do we realize just what God meant about working together as the body of Christ. No matter the circumstances, He never fails or forsakes us, we just need to wait for change to come knowing the battle has already been won. His promises still stand!

You see the devil doesn't want us to birth something that will destroy his kingdom. He pulled all stops to try to prevent me from writing this book, and believe me, on many occasions I wanted to give up. But I knew deep within my spirit that this book needed to be birthed no matter the pain. At the time of this writing I am sitting in bed recovering from Pneumonia. I have learnt that no matter my circumstances I count it all joy as I know God is working in me for my own good. Something good is around the corner! This book was birthed out of a desire to help you find your joy again, so you can get the understanding that God has been with you every step of the way. If my story can help you see that, then all the pain, toil, frustration, spiritual attacks and doubt will be worth it.

This book is a love letter from one mother to another. Let's take the journey toward healing together. Are you ready? Let's go...

2. Admitting Defeat

This is what the LORD says: Do not be afraid! Don't be discouraged by this mighty army, for the battle is not yours, but God's.

2 Chronicles 20:15

Sitting on the aeroplane we are about to take off. The kids are buckled in safely, and the air hostess starts her safety check and emergency demonstration. Not many passengers are paying attention as the voice on the loudspeaker reads the safety precautions. The hostess demonstrates how the oxygen masks will fall from the ceiling in case of emergency. The other passengers continue their idle chatter or settle down to sleep.

Did anyone actually catch that? Oxygen masks, say what? The first time it dawned on me I had to mull over the concept for a bit. The hostess clearly said that adults are to put the oxygen masks on themselves first, before helping their children! At first I thought she was joking, then after thinking it through it made total sense. How can I help my own children get their oxygen if I am starving for air and pass out? Drum roll please...

We are warriors in a war, we are the ones who have to find the strength in Jesus to be able to step up and stand up for our loved ones. But if we are constantly battling with ourselves, battling with the devil in our minds, getting pushed around in the boxing ring of life; how are we ever going to be effective for anybody else? Or for God's kingdom? First things first ladies and gentlemen, we need to sort out what is going on within ourselves before we can be effective evangelists, prayer warriors, influencers, mothers, wives, daughters, fathers, husbands, and sons. We need our oxygen masks first. No matter what destiny God has saved for you, you need to look internally first to clear out the junk that is blocking the flow of righteousness and peace that already belongs to you in Christ Jesus.

Praying for our children can definitely show us a lot about ourselves.

In my own situation, I asked myself if my child's behaviour was due to nurture or nature? I started to realize that there were some common traits that came from me and my family line. I felt so guilty when I realized the behaviour was a mirror of my own mistakes. I am so disappointed with myself and heart broken that I was part of the problem that created so many issues that affected my child's self-esteem. Deep within myself I knew that my child needed more help than I could provide. Even though I know that I have played a part I know that I am not entirely to blame, as there is a thing called free will. I spent years beating myself up about what I coulda-woulda-shoulda done, feeling helpless with no way out. I know that God is willing and able to forgive me and repair our hearts so He can make all things new. Throughout the whole ordeal I never felt like anyone was advocating for me, his mother. My child was hurting but so was I.

During the midst of all of this I would cry out to God; "Why are you allowing this to happen? What did I do wrong as a parent? Why am I being punished for this?" My knees have calluses on them from all the praying I did. I spent a solid nine months day after day constantly reading, praying and reciting the Word over my child and myself. I threw myself into learning everything I could about how the brain works, emotions, learning disabilities and drenching myself in God's Word. After that February trip I realized that things had come to a point where it needed an intervention. I could no longer ignore, hope, and pray that the situation would resolve itself. Immediately I dropped what I was doing, I stopped trying to hustle for clients, and focused on my family. As an entrepreneurial mom it is hard to step back from the hustle. I was so used to being on the treadmill of push, push, push, try, try, try, work, work, work. But this became my tipping point when physically my body was screaming at me to stop and take stock. I could no longer continue at this pace.

Then six weeks later, when we received the devastating news that my mother-in-law had passed away after a two-year battle with cancer, my life imploded. It was the straw that broke the camel's back. To say that my family was in shock is an understatement. It just felt like one emotional attack after the other. For a whole week I could not hold a conversation, and my mother and my sister would phone to see how I was doing, but I literally couldn't talk to them without crying so I had to text. This kind of physical grief took me completely by surprise. I have lost family members before, like my beloved grandparents, but I knew their time had come and I was at peace. Yet the shock of my mother-in-laws death triggered a waterfall of emotions and the dam walls that held my emotions inside had broke. Every feeling of regret, remorse, loss, anger, frustration, disappointment, and pain came flooding out. All I could do was let myself grieve and allow time to pass.

During that time of grief I realized that physically my body was screaming at me. After the years of stress and living on adrenalin it had taken its toll. I just needed to sleep, I needed to allow myself time to process through the emotions, without having any expectations or responsibility. I withdrew from friends and social media. It took a while for people to notice that I was not online posting as much. It was hard for me because I really do like to be positive. I am an encourager and exalter, I am the one that offers positive encouragement to others. Yet at the time I did not have anything left to give to others, I felt like I became the one who needed the encouragement.

Yet God in His goodness poured His encouragement into my soul. He is loving, He is patient, He is kind. He took me through the process of allowing me to go back to healing my inner self and my soul, so that I could be the effective mother, wife and prayer warrior that He destined me to be. But there was still work yet to be done. The biggest revelation to fixing my entire situation was love. It was that simple. Love myself, love my child and allow the healing love of God to flow in me and through me. It is not a weakness to admit that we feel defeated and need God to rescue us. It shows strength to be humble and honest and ask for help. I'm not qualified to run my own life and since I gave the reigns to Jesus I've never been happier!

My darling friend, if you are feeling frustrated with where you are at, and you know that you are destined for more, you are not alone. You want to do God's Kingdom work, yet you feel like you are stuck in the past. You are playing old records of disappointments, and you just cannot get past looking at yourself and your current situation. It is time you started to do some inner work on the internal issues so that you can graduate from focusing on yourself, to walking in your destiny to help others.

It is time you put your own oxygen mask on.

Helicopter Parent

Come to me, all who labor and are heavy laden, and I will give you rest.

Matthew 11:28

In today's society, many parents feel that we have to mollycoddle our children and be helicopter parents. We have to protect them from every little failure, every little fault, and every little hardship. Yet I have come to realize that this is not necessarily the right approach. I got bullied as a kid, and I never wanted my own children to experience that same pain and rejection. It is natural for us to want to protect our children, however I have learnt that there is value in those experiences. By enduring failure and being resistant we learn from our mistakes, and it actually is the most valuable life lesson we can learn.

Thinking back to when my children were babies, I had lots of patience with them while they were still growing up. When they became toddlers they learnt to walk, and yet I was fully prepared to let them fall down several times. As parents we let our kids step out and let them fall, because we are ready to pick them up and love them no matter what. When they misbehave, we teach them about the consequences of their behaviour. There is the practice of time out in the naughty chair which can be very effective!

Some of us parents (myself included) have developed this perfectionist mindset. This is especially true if we grew up with parents who were hard taskmasters, who always expected the best from us, and anything less than perfection was unacceptable. It is a very hard road to walk when you feel that nothing you do is ever good enough. Perhaps it was not our parents, perhaps it was ourselves. As women, we are very hard on ourselves. We have this high level of expectation of what we think the world demands of us; we need to be the perfect mother, perfect wife, perfect business owner, perfect homemaker. But perfection is a very hard taskmaster. As a recovered perfectionist, I have had to learn that some things are just best left alone, or some things are just worth accepting will never be done. Some things are not meant to be done, or are best done in some other way, shape or form (even if we do not reach perfection). What I mean by this, is that sometimes 80% finished is better than 100% with no action. None of us, other than Jesus, could ever aspire to be perfect in our lives, so why do we even try?

For me, procrastination has often been a big issue and obstacle, because I have always felt that I have been stuck in procrastination station waiting for the perfectionist ticket to allow me on the train. However, standing in the station being stuck is not a good way to learn and grow. It is only when I am moving and I actually get on the train and start taking steps towards my destiny, that I can make course adjustments. Even if I am on the wrong train, that does not matter, at least I am making progress.

What happened along the way? When our children were young we were patient to teach them that falling down and getting up is a good thing. Then as they grow our expectations change and we (and society) expect more and more from them. But what if our child is not ready to take those steps without assistance? This becomes very hard when this child is at an age when they "should" be performing at an expected level of maturity, especially when we start comparing them to their peers. What happens when our expectations are not met? We have become swept away with what the world says our children should be and do, that we beat ourselves up for their 'failings'. We are hard on them and harder on ourselves for not being there to pick them up when they fall. I think we need an attitude and perspective adjustment....

Love is the Foundation

Jesus answered: Love the Lord your God with all your heart, soul, and mind. This is the first and most important commandment. The second most important commandment is like this one. And it is, "Love others as much as you love yourself." All the Law of Moses and the Books of the Prophets are based on these two commandments.

Matthew 23:37-40

The basics of all break through is love. I know it sounds cliche but there is a reason. God said that the most important commandment is to love – love God first and love others like we love ourselves. Herein lies the problem. How can we love others when we cannot love ourselves? We cannot give away what we do not have. That is the crux of the matter. As a mother I would beat myself up about my failings and frailties that I put an impossible standard on my children. If I could not achieve perfection myself, why was I expecting perfection from my own children? This my friends, is exactly why we need to look at our own motivations, expectations and mindsets before we can put pressure on anyone else to perform.

The key is to love our rebellious children into the Kingdom just like Jesus did. He walked in love, accepted people where they were at, and came down to their level. He didn't say "Okay folks, once you clean up your act and stop doing all those sinful things, only then will I come to save you". No, He saves us just as we are!

A relationship is built on spending time together, understanding and acceptance. We cannot discipline our children into God's Kingdom because they will never be enough, do enough or know enough to pass our high standards of parenting perfection. Love opens the heavens over us and God can work in our lives if we give God the freedom to work, but if we stay in judgment and disagreement it will build blocks.

The Prodigal Promise

The Lord is not slow in keeping his promise, as some understand
slowness. Instead he is patient with you, not wanting anyone to perish,
but everyone to come to repentance.

2 Peter 3:9

Praying for a prodigal is very painful. We birth our children, they grow up, and we hope that they will follow the same path. But sometimes it doesn't happen that way. Even in the Bible, the story of the prodigal son is very very heartbreaking. To think that the son had everything that he wanted, a loving family who believed in him, every material blessing that he wanted; yet he still was not happy. Nothing has changed from those Bible days. We seem to have the same story, just on a different day. Many of our kids find that they get to the teenage years and start questioning their beliefs, their faith, and what their parents have taught them. But this could not necessarily be a bad thing. I personally think it is the way God made us, to be able to question things and to really push back and to seek understanding for ourselves. Is this truly something I believe? It is heartbreaking as a mother to see it happen, your child who you took to Bible school every week, who did Bible camps every year, all of a sudden decides it is not what they believe. But there is this thing called free will. We cannot force somebody to love us or to believe what we believe. They have to believe it for themselves.

The story of the prodigal is really a story of faith for parents holding on to that promise. Knowing that God wants our children to be saved, even if they do turn away. Whether they are teenagers, young adults, or even fully mature adults and still fighting their faith, feeling convicted that they once knew the Lord. Perhaps they were raised in an environment where they did not know the Lord, and now they just find themselves lost and astray. The biggest lesson I had to learn in this whole process is that the only way that the prodigal finds his way home is after he has been in the pig pen. I know, not a pretty thought, and it is something I had to really grapple with for a long time. Trying to save my own child from going to the pig pit was only delaying the healing process. It is only when they are at the bottom of the pit do they realize that they actually need help. If you notice in the bible story that only once the prodigal had to eat piggy slush, did he realize that he needed help. Only then (after all the partying, drugs, and rock and roll) did he decide that he needed to go back to his father's house. The big difference was that now he was humble. That pig pen taught him humility, taught him to appreciate what he had, so that when he did return home, he was there because it was his choice and his beliefs and his faith was then grounded. Keeping hold of that promise while our children are in the wilderness and behaving like a prodigal is hard for us parents to hold on to. This is especially true when you have those dark days when your child has been involved in all sorts of erroneous activities like drugs, addiction, depression etc. There is long laundry list of things that the devil tries to entice them with. All we can do is trust and pray.

What I have learnt from this whole process is that I cannot allow it to push the pause button on my own story. I cannot stop doing what I want to do with my own life or prevent myself from moving forward. I felt like I could not do anything further without this promise being fulfilled first. God showed me this and said, "You can't keep putting everything on pause while you are holding on waiting for your child to make the decision to turn back to me. You are using it as an excuse to delay doing what I told you to do, so just be obedient." I realized that my life has to go on. As hard as it is to let go and do what God has said, I found peace by letting Him do His thing. It really is something you have to think about daily, pray about fervently, and find the strength to continue walking out your faith even when you are in the midst of your storm. Be at peace knowing that all those prayers, all that love, and all that promise is going to come to pass in the right time, we just need to rely on the Lord in the waiting.

I'm sure many of you can recite the scripture in Proverbs 22:6...

Train up a child in the way he should go, and when he is old he will not depart from it.

I think this is really really true. We have to truly believe that if we have established a Godly foundation in the younger years, that when it comes to the important stage when a child starts questioning their faith, that they will remember their training. God will bring those scriptures to their remembrance and their training will not depart from them. But the caveat is for us to stand firm and to rely on the Lord. When a prodigal returns home and is reconciled with the people who love him or her, there is always a feast and a huge cause for celebration!

Guilt Trip

As far as the east is from the west, so far has He removed our transgressions from us.

Psalm 103:12

As a mother I constantly felt guilty about my situation. How could I let this happen to my child? Why did I not notice it earlier? What did I do wrong? All those feelings of guilt and condemnation came rushing at me like a freight train. I am a fixer and all I know is to step up and fix things. I did everything that I could to find a solution to our problem. First it was educational testing, a physical exam, blood tests, psychologist, a psychiatrist and a trial of medication. Yet we still had no concrete answers. We nurture, love and care for our children when they are born and yet we find ourselves in a situation we cannot control. Pack your bags we are going on a guilt trip!

As a society we are embarrassed with what others might think, so we keep the pain to ourselves and do not reach out for help. We think it will cause a neighborhood scandal if anyone found out that we are not the perfect family. Oh my, gosh can you imagine? Really people, who are we kidding! It is about time we shed those masks of perfection and got real. Who in the world has it perfect anyway?

It is about time we forgive ourselves. None of us are perfect parents, none of us have perfect kids. None of us have perfect lives. Yet we pile on the guilt. Especially us moms, we tend to compare ourselves to everybody else, and then that comparison steals our joy. Once our joy is lost we feel totally guilty about things that are not working the way they should. Honestly, forgiving ourselves is really the key to breaking out of the guilt prison. Because when we are guilty, we will do things that will either appease our kids, or enable them when we shouldn't. If we keep harassing ourselves with "what could I have done to prevent it? What part did I play? It is my fault it happened." We just perpetuate the cycle.

The old mix tape keeps going through our heads over and over and over, it just keeps playing that same broken record. It keeps us in the cycle of guilt that never really gets us moving forward. Using negative words like "what is wrong with you?" Or worse still "what is wrong with me?" isn't going to help you or your child. God does not want us to keep wallowing in guilt and condemnation, He wants us to know that we have forgiveness through Christ. Even though we may have done something wrong we can ask for forgiveness, we can move forward, and God can make everything new. But we have to choose to let go of that guilt and not use it either as a badge, or as a crutch. We may have become so used to feeling guilty that we feel guilty when we are not feeling guilty! It is about time we started being more aware of our feelings and our thoughts, so we can take action and really move ourselves past this stage into victory.

Free Will

Choose my instruction rather than silver, and knowledge rather than pure gold.

Proverbs 8:10

Control freaks anonymous. That is what we should call our blessed mom-worry club. Why do we find it so hard to let go and let God have His way? Perhaps it is because we do not truly trust God to do what He says He will do, or do it fast enough or to our liking. Come on now honey, admit it. You probably are already a member and did not know it!

In Joshua 24:15 it says...

But if serving the LORD seems undesirable to you, then choose for yourselves this day whom you will serve, whether the gods your ancestors served beyond the Euphrates, or the gods of the Amorites, in whose land you are living. But as for me and my household, we will serve the LORD."

Notice the word 'choose' is not a command. God gives us free will. He wants us to choose Him. He wants us to choose to do right. He will never force His will on us He is a gentleman. That is why we have the choice to decide what we believe and what we will do with our lives. God will never override our free will because we are not robots. He created us in His image, and He wants us to be with Him, and He wants us to choose Him. Just like it is with our own children, we cannot force them to love us or to choose our ways. We have to trust them to make the decision for themselves.

God will never override free will, but He will do His best to try to woo us into a love relationship. Before someone comes to know Christ, He shows them in different ways how He does love them, but often they are not paying attention to actually receive it. When it comes to our own children, knowing that they have free will, we have to come to peace that they may choose not to accept our beliefs. When they are little and they do not make the right choices, we can discipline them and steer them right. But when they come to an age of accountability, it is much harder to grasp this concept. This is especially hard when you know the choices they are making are actually hurting them.

All we can do is pray that God will impress upon their hearts His desire for their lives, that they will eventually choose the way to everlasting life. Once you choose something, and you make up your mind up, no one can stop you. If it is something that you did not necessarily choose for yourself, or if you are doing it for the wrong reasons (perhaps for someone else), it often does not last. It is like the seed that falls on concrete it dries up and dies. Unless it is a decision that you personally made on your own, for yourself, very rarely will that decision stick. For example, how many adults do you know who chose a field of study because of how much money they can earn or because of their parents expectations, only to find themselves miserable years later or in another field? Yes, way too many.

So what we can do is stay faithful to God, faithful to the promise that He knows that He will deliver our children, and deliver us out of our situation. We need to trust God by laying down our will at the feet of the cross and saying, "God, here I am. I give You my will. I want Your will for my life." It reminds me of what Jesus did in the garden when He said, "Take away this cup, but if it is not Your will..." He knew that what He had to go through would be really really hard, but He knew the Father's will was better than His own and He conceded His will. We could argue that Jesus suffered a lot and who in their right mind would willingly do that, but we know at the end of the day there was reason for His suffering. For someone who is selfish (aka teenagers) and walking in rebellion, it is a really hard concept to understand. All we can do is decide what we want for our own lives and pray for our children's lives by laying them at God's feet.

Cultural Cracks

Train up a child in the way he should go, and when he is old he will not depart from it.

Proverbs 22:6

We teach our kids what we know and what we think is true. We teach them to react to situations and display emotions by watching us. If we have an angry outburst they are going to be learning from us thinking, " if Mom and Dad became angry for that reason, then it is okay for me to be angry too". Our children learn to criticize, judge, and disparage one another through our parenting. Yes, I know it is hard to hear and admit, but we have taught our kids to think and believe what we believe, and often the results are not good. If we were raised in a violent, angry, and racial heated environment, the whole concept of nurture comes into being. It is really hard for a child not to think that their truth is THE truth if that is what your truth is, and your truth may have become tainted by your own bad parenting examples and experiences.

So we need to think clearly and carefully about how we might have erroneously taught our kids bad habits, that now show up in their behaviour. Whether it is getting angry in traffic or whether it is making racial remarks, or criticizing another culture that you do not understand; at the end of the day we all need to walk in repentance. Repentance for criticism, repentance for judgment, repentance for hatred, you name it the list can be long. When we walk in forgiveness, we can put our own parenting mistakes in the past because ignorance is not bliss. Not understanding and having a full comprehension of a situation can really create huge problems. If we have created a tense environment in our homes and now that our kids are older, we are finding they are behaving the same way, or in a way that we do not agree with, perhaps we need to look at ourselves first. What did we do in the parenting arena that might have taught them this behaviour?

Now honey do not get this twisted, I am not saying you have to get all guilty about past mistakes because we have talked about that already. What is so important is when we walk in love, we walk in tolerance and understanding. Sometimes as parents, we start judging our own kids based on things we do not understand. If a child is told time and time again that they are no good and that they are stupid, they are going to start believing it. How many times have you heard someone say "He was a bad kid I knew he was going to be trouble." That is not giving that poor kid a chance to prove what he is capable of because of the labels we put on him. If we do not take the time to look at someone else's viewpoint, we will only see one skewed angle. This can become a very sad situation when relationships get frayed and families break up.

Start a conversation, start to listen, and really hear what your loved one is saying. Sometimes our kids are telling us things, and we are not actually listening because we have a bias towards the way things should be. The more we can walk in love, the more we can walk in understanding, the better we will all be.

Flawed Parenting

For who has understood the mind of the Lord so as to instruct him?

But we have the mind of Christ.

I Corinthians 2:16

God wired our brains a certain way for a certain reason. Creative, multi dimensional thinkers are designed for a specific purpose, and often this means that they do not comply with the regular system. They do not fit into boxes, instead they are suffocated by them. In my situation, when my husband and I took the time to step back and understand our child, we reserved judgement so we could comprehend it for ourselves. This meant getting down on the child's level, looking at it from the child's point of view, showing love and understanding. How do we as parents manage an unimaginable situation that we have never been prepared of trained for? The advent of technology has bombarded our kids brains with more info on a daily basis than the president had access to twenty years ago! That parenting perfectionism comes into play again, "What will the neighbors think if my children do not behave? What if they think I do not have it all together and I am not perfect? " Oh heavens what a scandal! Let's face it, most of us parents are winging it. None of our kids arrived with operational manuals, we had to figure out their personality quirks as they grew. This is why trying to parent our children by following a strict set of 18th century rules, or a societal norms, may not work for today's 21st century child. A sign of maturity is to try to understand a situation from the other person's perspective for yourself, before allowing the opinions of others to sway your point of view. The truth of the matter is that we criticize what we do not understand. We hear the fear mongering about how bad too much screen time is for our kids, and yes I agree excess is not good for anyone. But what if we looked at WHY our kids react to this kind of stimulus so we can understand and parent them better? Reserve your judgement until you know all the facts.

Shatter the Silence

We destroy arguments and every lofty opinion raised against the knowledge of God, and take every thought captive to obey Christ.

2 Corinthians 10:5

There is a big elephant in the room and it remains nameless. Everybody knows that we have a problem, but no one is willing to talk about it. This is how disease spreads; by stealth and under the cover of darkness. Society has shamed us into thinking that it is not okay to talk about the tough issues in life, we are only supposed to show our highlight reels on social media. It is amazing when you hear of a family who has a child suffering from a life threatening disease, or when a family member passes away; that everyone rallies around them to support and help them. However, when we have a child or family member who is suffering from a mental illness, we are too ashamed to speak up and get support. The fact of the matter is that the silence gags honesty, stifles truth and kills progress. When we can be transparent enough to raise our hands and say "Hey I am struggling over here, please can someone help me?" that is when we win the war. If we are too embarrassed to talk about it nothing will ever change. Are you ready to break the silence and be brave enough to speak up and change your life, your family and the world?

Praying for our Children

And so I am willing to put up with anything. Then God's special people will be saved. They will be given eternal glory because they belong to Christ Jesus.

2 Timothy 2:10

Do you really trust God? Let's be honest, sometimes we doubt that God hears our prayers. It can feel like a dry, lonely, forgotten season when our knees are calloused from all the praying. Here is the deal... stop feeling shameful about your situation, go tell a friend and stand together and pray.

Matthew 18:20

For where two or three gather in my name, there am I with them.

Prayer truly is powerful. Imagine you have super powers and you are pushing back the evil forces with your words like a mighty gale force wind. When we pray we are agreeing with heaven, and like it says in the Lord's prayer "on earth as it is in heaven", we are ushering in heaven's will on earth. The key is to start with thanksgiving and praise, then make your requests known to God.

Psalm 100:4

Enter his gates with thanksgiving and his courts with praise; give thanks to Him and praise His name.

Keep it positive. No whining, complaining, pity parties or woe is me allowed. Get serious about what you want God to do, get down to business and ask nicely. I know this can be a hard one, but if we ask with confidence and then take back our requests because God is not answering us fast enough, we start the process all over again. Prayer and stand firm on the Word, even if it means printing out scriptures you can read every day to keep your faith strong. Let go and let God do His thing.

3. Barriers to Blessings

Barriers to Blessings

For when we died with Christ we were set free from the power of sin.

Romans 6:7

Martin Luther sparked the Protestant Reformation (1) on October 31, 1517 when he nailed his "95 Theses" to the door of the Wittenberg Castle church. He was committed to the idea that salvation could be attained only through faith and by divine grace only. Luther vigorously objected to the Catholic Church corrupt practice of selling indulgences.

Just like Martin Luther, we too need to nail our sins and transgressions to the cross because Jesus already died to forgive them and absolve us from all punishment. No amount of good behaviour or "works" will save us because we have already been saved by grace, which is a free gift available to all.

The problem with humanistic view of "self improvement" is that there are limits to our self. We are finite beings with limits to our energy and effectiveness. Relying on ourselves to "be strong" or "you can do it" without God, is severely limiting our potential. That is the beauty of the gospel because we are a hot mess without Jesus. No amount of willpower or hard work will change our situation if we omit the one person who has the keys to it all, Jesus.

In the story of Jesus healing the paralyzed man his friends lowered him through the roof because it was packed and no one was coming through the door. The faith of his friends inspires me that even though they were turned away at first, they persisted and broke down the roof so their friend would get healed.

Mark 2 :1-5

1 When He had come back to Capernaum several days afterward, it was heard that He was at home. 2 And many were gathered together, so that there was no longer room, not even near the door; and He was speaking the word to them. 3 And they came, bringing to Him a paralytic, carried by four men. 4 Being unable to get to Him because of the crowd, they removed the roof above Him; and when they had dug an opening, they let down the pallet on which the paralytic was lying. 5 And Jesus seeing their faith said to the paralytic, "Son, your sins are forgiven."

Reading the story I thought "how fabulous this man gets healed because of his faith". But did you notice something fascinating? Jesus turned to him and said "Your sins are forgiven" then he was healed, not "be healed" like he had many times before. Why did he needs sins forgiven and why was he paralyzed because of his sins? The plot thickens... Here is a thought to bring things into perspective. Sometimes we are afflicted and we may not know why or the source. Sometimes it could be due to our past sins that we have inadvertently committed and the consequences are sickness, destruction and captivity.

James 4:7

Submit yourselves, then, to God. Resist the devil, and he will flee from you.

If you have been feeling stuck, suffer from self doubt or anxiety, are dealing with fear, have a low self esteem etc.; these are all symptoms of a deeper root. Unless we deal with the root cause we will continue to repeat the same habits and characteristics. We are going to delve deeper into these root causes in more detail so you can mine out any offending items that might be blocking your blessings, and be the source of the barriers to your breakthrough. Let us get ready to let your light shine!

Heartbroken

He heals the brokenhearted and binds up their wounds.

Psalm 147:3

There is an ancient Japanese art called Kintsugi (2) known as "the art of precious scars". It teaches that broken objects are not something to hide but to display with pride. This traditional 15th century Japanese art uses a precious metal like liquid gold, liquid silver or lacquer dusted with powdered gold, to bring together the broken pieces of a pottery item. The technique consists of joining the fragments together and giving them a new, more refined look that enhances the breaks. Every repaired piece is unique due to the random nature of the way ceramics shatters, and the irregular patterns formed are enhanced with the use of metals. The final product looks like a piece of gilded art with golden veins throughout the repaired piece. Each piece has its own unique story and beauty. The most impressive aspect to the art is that once the pottery is repaired it is far stronger than it was before. The Kintsugi technique suggests that we should not just throw away broken objects as it doesn't mean that it is no longer useful. Instead, the breakages can become valuable.

Our hearts are created whole and every experience (both good and bad) leaves a mark. If you could imagine your heart looked like a pretty vase perfectly shaped by the potter's hands. Every groove, curve and angle designed by the master artist to display the beauty of His creation. We are born to serve to give God glory and all that He places in our care. However every hurt, every blow, and every fall can leave a crack in our beautiful vase. If left unattended the vase will become so fragile and brittle it will disintegrate and eventually fall to pieces. Our natural inclination is to simply throw the broken pieces away.

People can die from a broken heart. Often times it is the pain of loss that leaves a void that seems impossible to fill, when the person eventually gives up on life. Each of us should look at our traumatic experiences in a positive way, as a way of learning from the negative. This is the true essence of resilience. It is our experiences that makes each person unique, beautiful and precious. In God's eyes this is exactly how He sees us. God repairs us with valuable gold and the result is priceless. You are not trash but an art piece ready to be displayed for the world to see!

The Mind is the Battlefield

For we wrestle not against flesh and blood, but against principalities, against powers, against the rulers of the darkness of this world, against spiritual wickedness in high places.

Ephesians 6:12

Have you had one of those days that seem to go from bad to worse? Like it never rains but pours? One bad thing after another? Often times it is a result of our own bad attitude and choices, and sometimes it is no fault of your own. But sometimes it is the enemy who is trying to steal your joy and peace.

The place the enemy likes to attack us first is our minds, then he goes for our emotions. If he can get us to question our purpose, our calling, our destiny; he can stop us from walking out the plan God has for our lives and our loved ones. As soon as we recognize the minefield trap that is our cranky teenager who throws insults, or that petulant child who refuses to listen, or the siblings who insist on arguing; we can learn to detect an attack of division and discord immediately amongst the ranks, and prevent it from derailing our day and our destiny.

The enemy uses stealth, confusion, distraction, and frustration to cloak his strategy. He moves slow and steady, under the cover of darkness so you cannot detect him. He is so lame he only has three agendas that do not change: steal, kill, destroy. He cannot create or come up with anything original, he is a total faker and copycat. If we can open our spiritual eyes we will soon be able to detect his attacks before they can destroy us. That punk devil is a pathological liar with sticky little fingers always trying to poke you in the eye and blind you to his schemes!

If we can rise above and stay in praise like David did after the battle of Ziklag, we too can rise above when we have learnt to recognize the battle strategy. If you do not know the story of David and Ziklag let me explain. So David and his army conquered their enemy and when they returned home to their families they found the enemy had burned down their homes and kidnapped their wives and children. Can you imagine? Total freak fest... His army soon became angry and can you guess what they did next? They became furious and turned on David and division set in.

1 Samuel 30 :1-6

1 David and his men reached Ziklag on the third day. Now the Amalekites had raided the Negev and Ziklag. They had attacked Ziklag and burned it, 2 and had taken captive the women and everyone else in it, both young and old. They killed none of them, but carried them off as they went on their way. 3 When David and his men reached Ziklag, they found it destroyed by fire and their wives and sons and daughters taken captive. 4 So David and his men wept aloud until they had no strength left to weep. 5 David's two wives had been captured—Ahinoam of Jezreel and Abigail, the widow of Nabal of Carmel. 6 David was greatly distressed because the men were talking of stoning him; each one was bitter in spirit because of his sons and daughters. But David found strength in the LORD his God.

Most country western movies have some element of insurrection when the going gets tough, and usually people start to question their hope and their God. The leader gets thrown under the bus and is blamed for all things that go wrong. Divide and conquer, it is a common strategy the enemy loves to use. But can you guess what broke the back of the insurrection and division and helped David and his army win the battle? He stayed in praise. David remained focused on God (not the drama), he focused on praise and worship (not the petty bickering). God then downloaded a divine strategy that gave him clarity and a strategy to win the war.

If we can stop the enemy from winning the battle in our minds, we can stop him in his tracks from winning the war. The smartest thing we can do is recognize the attack, focus on God and not give up. God has said we are already conquerors, so do not concede defeat simply because you do not think you can win. If you really believed that you could not lose, wouldn't you go in the fight confidently knowing that the God of all the universe has already given you the victory?

Romans 8:37...

No, in all these things we are more than conquerors through him who loved us.

Then it is about time we take up our prize, step up and claim what is rightfully ours. The first step is to take captive those thoughts of insurrection that are trying to derail your progress by learning to recognize what is of God, your own ramblings and the enemy. Just imagine the battle cry you would give out when you are confident that the weapons you have at your disposal are already primed in your favour to win!

Learning to discern will become one of the strongest tools in your arsenal and the only way to sharpen the blade of truth is to know the truth. Once you know the original you will recognize the fake, the fraud, the phony. It is important to dismiss those ramblings that are designed to take you down by stealth as soon as they pop into your head to make you question yourself. If you do not know the strategy you are already defeated. Once you know the strategy you can aim your darts at the bullseye and take down the enemy's weapons with precision.

Close your eyes for a minute... (okay maybe after you have read this section). Imagine you're standing in a field that is blurred by fog, you cannot see ten steps ahead of you. You sense there is something out there, but because you cannot see ahead of you, you are frozen in fear, too scared to take a step toward victory. Okay you can open your eyes now... Let us imagine that you had the knowing all along that even though there is fog, that there is a safe grassy green you can walk through without fear of disaster? Even though the fog surrounds you, if you had the knowledge that it is only temporary and that you have the tools to clear the fog, would you still stand in fear? No you would not.

You my dear would be standing tall, weapons in hand, ready to take on what hides behind the fog. You know that you are not walking by sight, but by the confidence and power that God has given you as His child. The good news is that you have already won the war, you just need to be brave enough to step up and take hold of it. Take possession of your promised land! The great news is that all of heaven are behind you as the heavenly hosts stand waiting for you to take up your inheritance. The better news is that no matter your age your mind can be re-trained. If you have suffered from "stinking thinking" all your life you can take out the trash and clean up house. We are going to clean out the areas of your life that you have knowingly or unknowingly opened yourself up to to be harassed by the enemy. Get ready to take back authority and activate the blessings in our life. Let us get ready to fight!

Soul Wounds

We are afflicted in every way, but not crushed; perplexed, but not driven to despair; persecuted, but not forsaken; struck down, but not destroyed; always carrying in the body the death of Jesus, so that the life of Jesus may also be manifested in our bodies.

2 Corinthians 4:8-10

Have you noticed that when you are driving if you glance up at the sky the clouds look set, but when you stop and focus on one specific area you can see the clouds moving? Slaying the giants in our minds is often a matter of perspective. When we stand on the rock of Jesus everything looks small, but when we stay low in self pity or self loathing looking up everything looks big. We need to take a rest stop for us to see how God is moving in our life.

We are a three part being: spirit, body and soul. Our soul is made up of our mind, our will and emotions. When we are saved our spirit is instantly transformed, renewed and made whole through the redeeming power and saving grace of Christ's sacrifice. However the soul (the mind, will and emotions) are not instantly transformed. Instead we have to work through a healing process that works our spirit out through our soul, and eventually shows up in our body. It can be a confusing thing to grasp and many have grappled with this concept, or even rejected the idea that we are not made entirely new at our moment of salvation. When we are saved we become an adopted child of God with an instant inheritance. This includes being whole and healed, but it is up to us to claim that inheritance. God knit us in our mother's womb and knows our innermost parts, and He is not surprised with us at all when He saves us. He knows what we have experienced, the hurts we have endured and the scars we carry. Because He loves us so much He wants us to be healed, whole and healthy.

3 John 2:2 (NKJV)

Beloved, I pray that you may prosper in all things and be in health, just as your soul prospers.

The key is to ask God to shine His torchlight on specific areas in your soul so that you can cleanse all darkness and allow Christ's resurrection power to heal you. This will enable you to walk in freedom, faith and your ultimate destiny. Speaking God's word out loud repeatedly while using all of your senses is how your soul catches up with your spirit.

Romans 10:17

Consequently, faith comes from hearing the message, and the message is heard through the word about Christ.

Psychologists say that our emotions are the last to catch up when we make a change to our behaviour. So be warned you won't 'feel' like doing it, you won't 'feel' strong enough to push through, and you won't 'feel' like there is any change. Make the decision right now not to be ruled by your emotions but to believe what the Word of God says about you. Eventually when things are worked through your soul, they will show themselves up as evidence. Keep the faith and be determined that you are going to do the work because God said He wants you to be blessed, healed and whole.

Author and speaker Katie Souza offers amazing resources for soul work. As a former drug dealer who spent time in prison her testimony is a true reflection of how God can take someone's life and totally turn it around for His glory. In her book "Healing the Wounded Soul" (3) Katie explains the concept of the 'dunamis' power that we as Christians all have access to. By now you know that I am half Greek, and every time I hear someone refer to a word that originates from Greek I get all excited. The reason is that the Greek language is rich with words that refer to a variety of meanings. Many direct translations do not correlate to an exact English word, but in this case there is reason to celebrate. The Greek word "dunamis" means "strength, power, or ability" and is used 121 (4) times in the New Testament. This is the root of the English words dynamite, dynamo and dynamic. How is that for awesome! It is important to note that dunamis is not just any power; the word often refers to 'miraculous power or marvelous' works especially with reference to the ministry of Jesus. Dunamis refers to "moral power and excellence of soul" according to Thayer's Greek Lexicon. Woo hoo dunamis is our superpower juice yay God! The key verses that refer to dunamis are Luke 1:35, Luke 4:36, Acts 1:8, Romans 1:20, 1 Corinthians 1 :22-24, 2 Corinthians 4:7, 2 Corinthians 12:9, Ephesians 3:20-21, 2 Timothy 1:7, Hebrews 1:3, and 2 Peter 1:3.

Dunamis is the resurrection power that enabled Jesus to perform His many miracles and the same power that raised Him from the dead. Now here is the most fantastic news ever, wait for it.... wait for it.... YOU have that same dunamis power living in you right now! From the moment you asked Jesus into your heart you had access to it. Whoosh mind blown right? We have the same authority through Christ and we can activate the dunamis power to work miracles in our lives. The most important part is that dunamis can refer to "inherent power, power residing in a thing by virtue of its nature, or which a person or thing exerts and puts forth" (ibid.). In Matthew 22:29 Jesus tells the Sadducees, "You are in error because you do not know the Scriptures or the power of God." Jesus has inherent power residing in Him because dunamis is part of His nature. When we become Christians we receive the same dunamis power because Jesus in 1 John 14 :12-23 says...

12 Very truly I tell you, whoever believes in me will do the works I have been doing, and they will do even greater things than these, because I am going to the Father. 13 And I will do whatever you ask in my name, so that the Father may be glorified in the Son. 14 You may ask me for anything in my name, and I will do it. 15 "If you love me, keep my commands. 16 And I will ask the Father, and he will give you another advocate to help you and be with you forever— 17 the Spirit of truth. The world cannot accept him, because it neither sees him nor knows him. But you know him, for he lives with you and will be in you. 18 I will not leave you as orphans; I will come to you. 19 Before long, the world will not see me anymore, but you will see me. Because I live, you also will live. 20 On that day you will realize that I am in my Father, and you are in me, and I am in you. 21 Whoever has my commands and keeps them is the one who loves me. The one who loves me will be loved by my Father, and I too will love them and show myself to them." 22 Then Judas (not Judas Iscariot) said, "But, Lord, why do you intend to show yourself to us and not to the world?" 23 Jesus replied, "Anyone who loves me will obey my teaching. My Father will love them, and we will come to them and make our home with them.

As Christians we do not live in our own power but in God's power He freely gives to us. In verse 12 it says "they will do even greater things" which means Jesus wants us to perform even greater miracles than He did of healing the sick, delivering people from demons, and raising people from the dead. Wowza how is that for wonder working power? It is God's ability that makes us able to accomplish anything of value, for apart from Him we can do nothing (John 15:5). It is His strength that makes us overcomers because we tap into the power we have through the Holy Spirit who resides in us by using the name of Jesus (verse 14).

Did you notice a few things that are keys to us activating this power? In verse 15 it says "If you love me keep my commands" and verse 21 "whoever has my commands and keeps them" an again verse 23 " anyone who loves me will obey my teaching". The big neon sign is pointing to us keeping commands and obedience. Without obedience there is no activation.

Hosea 4:6 says...

My people perish for lack of knowledge.

Too many Christians are living haphazard, lackluster, defeated lives because of the lack of knowledge of the inheritance we have in Christ. Is it not time we claimed our inheritance and walked in the dynamic power of Jesus? It is time we take a spiritual shower and cleanse our souls from the dirt, and remove the blockages from us walking in spirit and truth, so we can make claim to the dunamis power living in us!

Baby Steps

Truly I tell you, whatever you bind on earth will be bound in heaven, and whatever you loose on earth will be loosed in heaven.

Matthew 18 :18

Confession time I have to be honest. As I sit here writing this book I have not always enjoyed the process. It is dark and cold outside, no one is awake and my bed keeps calling me back to lullaby land. Initially when God laid the idea on my heart about writing this book I was all excited, but when it came to executing, the process became hard. I had to decide that I was in it for the long haul and that I would make the time and sacrifices it needed to get this baby birthed. I have had to sacrifice time with my family, I have stepped back from a volunteer role that would take up my weekends, I have forced myself to get to bed early so I can rise early, and disciplined myself to crunch two uninterrupted hours everyday to get my book written. The good news is that it is only for a season and I know the end result will be totally worth it! Writing a book is like birthing a baby; it is all exciting in the beginning, then nausea sets it, then you realize it is going to be a long wait, then it gets uncomfortable, then when it comes time to birthing the baby it is so flipping painful!

Breakthrough takes work and is not always the most pleasant, enjoyable or pretty process. Put that on your bumper sticker baby! The world is littered with empty promises, get rich quick schemes, easy fix shortcuts, and microwave mentalities. We all want it fixed and we want it now! But that is not how things work in the real world, just look at nature. God designed the seasons to ebb and flow and when we plant a seed, we do not get an immediate tree pop out the ground. We plant the seeds then we have to show patience in watering and feeding that seed. Growth takes time but gradually, little by little, the seed gets stronger to when it eventually breaks through the ground and kisses the sunlight.

When I first started on this healing process God gave me a vision. Driving in a car God is in the driver's seat and I am sitting next to him asking "Are we there yet? Are we there yet?". God turns to me and says "Stop nagging me, I have heard you, but there is a journey we need to take before we get there, so trust Me and be patient." Oops sorry God, my bad.

When you allow God to take you through the healing process it will take time and it will take work. Do not expect to say a prayer and beep out comes a ready made popcorn bag of blessings. If you have taken years to develop stinking thinking and bad habits, it will take time to heal and create new habits. Think of it as God gently dressing your wounds with antibacterial, and gently removing the stickiness. If He ripped off the bandaid in one shot it would be super painful! Be patient, do the work and trust God to take you through the healing process so you come out completely healed on the other side.

The other thing to note is that by having a tight fist holding onto things of old, we crush what we are squeezing, and are not open to receiving the new. New wine can only go into new wineskins, old skins cannot hold the new wine because the new skins will be destroyed.

Mark 2:22

And no one pours new wine into old wineskins. Otherwise, the wine will burst the skins, and both the wine and the wineskins will be ruined. No, they pour new wine into new wineskins.

We need to allow God to develop new skins (or containers) in us so we can receive his blessings by allowing the old to perish and die. This is the painful part, dying to self.

Galatians 2:20

I have been crucified with Christ and I no longer live, but Christ lives in me. The life I now live in the body, I live by faith in the Son of God, who loved me and gave himself for me.

Only when we truly relent can we receive because the new is so much better than we could imagine. But we have to trust God like the good Father that He is, to give us what we really need. If you have had a bad example of a father figure you might assume God is the same, but we have to trust the scriptures and learn what kind of loving Father He really is. Like a good father God needs to discipline us where necessary to keep us from hurting ourselves and others. God promises that we will occupy new territory, new land, a promised land.

What I found helpful is to use a journal to write down my thoughts, feelings and what I am sensing the Lord is saying to me. This is an important key to helping you celebrate the small wins as you document and track your progress. The other great thing is that you can look back in time and see how God has answered your prayers. Without some way to measure your progress you will soon find yourself disheartened and you may want to give up. So give yourself the best chance of success by starting out right. If you have taken years to think and feel the way you do, it will take time to work through the process.

Just like the story of Lazarus, Jesus brought him back to life in an instant but he still had his grave clothes to shed. Layer by layer, little by little, baby steps toward the finish line. Be kind to yourself, if you need more time then go back and re-read a section. Make notes of the things God places on your heart so you can saturate your soul with spiritual food in those areas. This may mean that you need to enlist the help of someone else, a trusted friend or counselor. Having somebody you can be accountable to will help keep you motivated when the going gets tough, and will encourage you to stay the course when things get rough.

The key thing to note is that much of the wrong thinking you have had is a result of old buried roots that were planted many years before. We have to dig out the roots to fix the fruit or your tree will keep blossoming rotten fruit that never becomes nourishment to you or anyone else. I am sure you have known someone who is just plain bitter, they are not nice to be around and generally put a damper on everyone's mood. Let us not let that spoil the fruit of what could be a vineyard ready for new healthy wine.

Note: Download the workbook that accompanies this book so you can take notes for the following sections by going to www.mimikacooney.com/warrior **(5)**

Our Helper

Do you not know that your bodies are temples of the Holy Spirit, who is in you, whom you have received from God? You are not your own;

1 Corinthians 6:19

There is a lot we can learn from Jesus when He walked the earth. During

Jesus's ministry He had a four part agenda which gives us the example to follow:

(1) Heal the sick, (2) Raise the dead, (3) Cleanse the lepers, (4) Cast out demons.

Matthew 10:7-8

7 As you go, proclaim this message: 'The kingdom of heaven has come near.' 8 Heal the sick, raise the dead, cleanse those who have leprosy, drive out demons. Freely you have received; freely give.

Just before Jesus ascended into heaven He shared this:

John 14:12

Very truly I tell you, whoever believes in me will do the works I have been doing, and they will do even greater things than these, because I am going to the Father.

Jesus left us with the Holy Spirit to enable us to do even greater works than He did. As you can see we have got work to do! The great news is that we can take back our authority through Jesus and by the guidance of the Holy Spirit who lives in us. He is our comforter, supporter and friend. That gentle voice you hear whispering softly the good things you know are true, like that you are loved, you are valued and you can do this. The Holy Spirit is your built in cheerleader always there to cheer you on. When in doubt ask the Holy Spirit what you should do or what God says about the situation because He is God!

In the following sections we are going to turn down the static noise of defeat that has been pushing a negative frequency by drowning out the junk. We are going to turn up the volume of the positive voice of the Holy Spirit so you walk forward in victory!

Roots

A good tree cannot bear bad fruit, and a bad tree cannot bear good fruit.

Matthew 7:18

Growing up in South Africa on twelve acres of land I have fond memories of my Papou (Greek Grandfather) tending our home grown garden patch. He had this awesome blue truck that he would use to till the soil and get it ready for planting. My favourite part was sitting on his lap helping him steer. The smell of the fresh African earth still lingers in my memory. Once the soil was cleared of debris and the plowing was complete, then it came time to planting the seeds. I would get all excited with the variety of options, the paper packets had pictures on them of what the final product should look like. One day while playing with the seed packets I accidentally got them mixed up. The labels had peeled off and now there was no way to know what was what. The only thing we could do was plant them and wait to see what would eventually germinate. The waiting was excruciating, everyday after school for weeks I would check on the seedlings to try and guess what they were. Eventually once the stems grew large enough Papou could recognize what vegetable we could expect to grow. By then the seeds had fully germinated and the plants were established, all they needed was water, sunshine and time.

Seeds are tricky little things because at first glance they look unimpressive and tiny. What can come from such a itty bitty thing? We cannot see what potential the seed has within it, yet God knows how many apples are in a seed. I remember my mother quoting the saying "one rotten apple ruins the barrel" especially when it came to picking my friends. Well this is very true, particularly when it comes to talking about our faith. We may have a beautiful looking tree with great big branches but when we pick the fruit and see it is rotten inside, it usually starts to infect the rest.

A good tree bears good fruit, and a bad tree bears bad fruit. If the roots are bad; no amount of watering, sunshine or fertilizer will turn the bad tree into a good one. Today there are many many professing Christians who are bearing bad fruit. They are saved by grace, they are forgiven, yet their lives are a sad depiction of what life in the spirit should look like. Now do not get your panties in a bunch, I am not saying you have to be "perfect" that is getting all legalistic. What I am saying is that they are losing out on all the promises that are rightfully theirs because they are not dealing with roots issues that are poisoning their lives.

Let's look at this scripture again in context:

Matthew 7:16-20

16 By their fruit you will recognize them. Do people pick grapes from thorn bushes, or figs from thistles? 17 Likewise, every good tree bears good fruit, but a bad tree bears bad fruit. 18 A good tree cannot bear bad fruit, and a bad tree cannot bear good fruit. 19 Every tree that does not bear good fruit is cut down and thrown into the fire. 20 Thus, by their fruit you will recognize them.

Roots that are left long enough grow stronger with time and are harder to uproot, so it is a good idea to take action early before it becomes a big problem. Many conditions, behaviours and circumstances are the symptoms of deeper issues. We can cut off the branches and the fruit, but if the root is left behind, the same problem will persist. The good news is that even if you have a big old oak tree growing in the garden of your heart, you can still uproot it with Jesus's help. After all He is the master gardener!

The Bible has many references of roots; Mark 11:20, Luke 17:6 , Ezekiel 31:7, Ezekiel 17:6, Ezekiel 17:9 , Jeremiah 17:8, Isaiah 14:29, Job 18:16, 1 Timothy 6:10, Isaiah 5:24, Isaiah 40:24.

Jesus said I am the vine and you are the branches and we are to be 'rooted' in Christ. This is one of my favourites;

In John 15:5 Jesus said,

"I am the vine; you are the branches. If you remain in me and I in you, you will bear much fruit; apart from me you can do nothing."

This means that if we 'ground' our faith and beliefs in what Jesus says, then we will bear good fruit and the 'fruits' of the spirit can only be love, joy, peace, kindness, goodness, long suffering etc. If we have planted our seed of faith in Jesus, then watered it with God's Word, allowed the light of Christ to shine and warm it; it will eventually grow into a beautiful tree for all to see. Trees have many uses especially when it comes to feeding others. A good tree that bears good fruit feeds and nourishes the birds and the people who pass by to enjoy it. If we do not know the root of a problem how can we address it? There are some major spiritual roots that we will be discussing in further detail that grow trees that grow branches which develop bad fruit. We need to uproot them so they do not infest the rest of our lives, or infect our children and generational line.

Trauma

"They hit me," you will say, "but I'm not hurt! They beat me, but I don't feel it!

Proverbs 23:25

According to the Merriam-Webster dictionary **(6)** the word "trauma" means; an injury (such as a wound) to living tissue caused by an extrinsic agent, a disordered psychic or behavioural state resulting from severe mental or emotional stress or physical injury, an emotional upset, an agent, force, or mechanism that causes trauma. The Greek word "traumatizó" **(7)** is where we get the word trauma from and means a wound.

According to research **(8)** Childhood trauma leads to lifelong chronic illness. Researchers at Yale **(9)** had recently shown that "child abuse, depression, and methylation in genes is involved with stress, neural plasticity, and brain circuitry." This means that when inflammatory stress hormones flood a child's body and brain, they alter the genes that oversee our stress reactivity (fight or flight), thereby re-setting the stress response to always be "high" or in stress mode for life. Stress increases the risk of inflammation, which is the cause of many diseases, and manifests later in life in cancer, heart disease, allergies, and autoimmune diseases.

The Huffington post article **(10)** goes on to say "People who'd experienced four such categories of childhood adversity (physical, emotional, sexual, or mental) were twice as likely to be diagnosed with cancer and depression as adults. Women who have faced three types of childhood adversity had a sixty percent greater risk of being hospitalized with an autoimmune disease as an adult. Similar links existed between childhood stressors and adult heart disease, diabetes, migraines and irritable bowel syndrome. Suffering six categories of early life stress shortens one's lifespan by twenty years." **(11)** Wow isn't that scary! Trauma is the door opener and root cause to many cases of premature death.

One study **(12)** of 125,000 patients showed that when physicians acknowledged and discussed a patients childhood trauma openly, patients enjoyed a thirty-five percent reduction in doctor visits. Validating a patients suffering invites patients to address the cause of their pain and move forward in healing their body and their soul.

Results of another study **(13)** showed that more than half of respondents reported at least one, and one-fourth reported more than two categories of childhood exposures to trauma. They found a graded relationship between the number of categories of childhood exposure to trauma and each of the adult health risk behaviours and diseases that were studied. According to the CDC, the annual health care costs **(14)** of adult patients who have a history of early trauma is $124 billion a year.

The results show that any kind of trauma we experience either in childhood or later in life can affect our health physically, mentally, emotionally and spiritually. Trauma becomes a barrier to us receiving the blessing of good health that Jesus died for us to have. The good news is that Jesus is the ultimate healer and can heal every crevice of brokenness you have in your heart, body and soul. It starts with acknowledgement, forgiveness and walking out your healing by saturating your soul in God's healing Word.

James 5:16

Therefore confess your sins to each other and pray for each other so that you may be healed. The prayer of a righteous person is powerful and effective.

No matter the kind of trauma you have experienced, there is no greater pain than for God to see His children wounded and hurting. God's Word is clear about His will for your complete healing and how He wants you to be set free. The great news is that Jesus did it all for us! God made the ultimate sacrifice and sent His only Son to die for you so you do not have to stay wounded. Through Jesus's blood sacrifice we can wipe our slates clean and be completely healed and redeemed as if we had never been hurt.

Isaiah 53:5

But he was pierced for our transgressions, he was crushed for our iniquities; the punishment that brought us peace was on him, and by his wounds we are healed.

In order to be healed of trauma we are to refuse to put up with it (decide to be set free), confess our sins to one another (repent of unforgiveness), and receive the gift of healing through Jesus's sacrifice (accept it as a gift).

Prayer: Healing from Trauma

Dear Lord thank you for sending your Son to die on the cross for me. Thank you that the blood Jesus spilt cleanses me and sets me free. As an act of my will I choose to release the pain of my past trauma and ask for You to forgive my sin of unforgiveness. I receive the gift of healing through Jesus's death and resurrection. I release the dunamis power of healing into all areas of my body and soul. Thank You for my complete healing in Jesus name amen!

Sins

God made him who had no sin to be sin for us, so that in him we might become the righteousness of God.

2 Corinthians 5:21

According to Wikipedia **(15)** the seven deadly sins are pride, greed, lust, envy, gluttony, wrath and sloth. We wound ourselves by the sins we commit. Looking deeper closer at the list of seven they include adultery (lust), fornication (lust), gossiping (pride and envy), drinking or eating excessively (gluttony), idolatry (lust and pride), emotional outbursts (pride and wrath), taking offense (pride, wrath and envy), laziness (sloth) etc. Sins of any kind can wound you especially the habitual kind that have become part of your personality. When you sin against yourself or against someone else your soul gets wounded. Our conscience also means soul, a lack of conscience will negatively affect our decisions and quality of life.

1 Corinthians 8:12

When you sin against them in this way and wound their weak conscience, you sin against Christ.

The reason I know your soul needs healing is because we are all wounded. A big way we hurt ourselves and others is through our words. Gossip or speaking evil against someone is considered slanderous and creates "deadly wounds" within our souls.

Proverbs 26:22

The words of a gossip are like choice morsels; they go down to the inmost parts.

If you want to live a life of freedom and If you do not want to be wounded and get sick, stop talking about people! Gossip is highly addictive, and so it complaining.

Jude 1:16

These people are grumblers and fault finders; they follow their own evil desires; they boast about themselves and flatter others for their own advantage.

Matthew 15:18

But the things that come out of a person's mouth come from the heart, and these defile them.

The soul wounds affect our personality and determine how we speak and who we become. A person's tainted language is a sign of a wounded soul. The Greek word for heart is "cardia" **(16)** which is where we get the word cardiac from means "the affective center of our being" and the capacity of moral preference". It is used over 800 times in scripture. Our mouths are the fountain that pours out the pain that lies deep within our souls, as out of the mouth the heart speaks. Enduring trauma like divorce, a car accident, death in the family, abuse, or loss wounds the soul. Generational iniquities also cause soul wounds, these are habitual sins committed by our ancestors that we may not know about.

Deuteronomy 5:9 (NLT)

You must not bow down to them or worship them, for I, the LORD your God, am a jealous God who will not tolerate your affection for any other gods. I lay the sins of the parents upon their children; the entire family is affected–even children in the third and fourth generations of those who reject me.

Iniquity is what we refer to as generational sin where rebellion and idolatry are considered a trespass. But we can see from the scripture above that if our ancestors rebelled against God and worshipped idols, it is caused them to be cursed, which then affects the third and fourth generation.

Psalm 51:5

Surely I was sinful at birth, sinful from the time my mother conceived me.

Greek word for womb is "koilia" **(17)** which also means "the innermost part of a man, the soul, heart" . You can be born with soul wounds that will make you physically sick as shown in this story about the lame man.

Soul wounds control emotions and can make you fearful, anxious, angry, and depressed. If you find yourself constantly fretting, complaining, worried, annoyed, discontented, argumentative, creating conflicts and drama, judgmental, or critical; then these are signs that your soul is deeply wounded. Families break up over soul wounds that infect the minds and hearts and eventually cause discord and division. Soul wounds affect your ability to prosper financially. Think of it this way, how can God bless you to steward finances successfully if you are wounded and blinded by hurt? Those hurts and wounds will affect your decision making process and your motives will be wrong.

Proverbs 11:25

A generous person will prosper; whoever refreshes others will be refreshed.

3 John 1:2 (NASB)

Beloved, I pray that in all respects you may prosper and be in good health, just as your soul prospers.

"Skotos" **(18)** in Greek means "darkness". The explanation means "of ignorance respecting divine things and human duties, and the accompanying ungodliness and immorality, together with their consequent misery in hell, persons in whom darkness becomes visible and holds sway." The good news is that by shining the light on the areas of darkness, we can illuminate and heal those soul wounds through Jesus.

Isaiah 30:26

The moon will shine like the sun, and the sunlight will be seven times brighter, like the light of seven full days, when the LORD binds up the bruises of his people and heals the wounds he inflicted.

Prayer: Forgiveness of Sins

Lord Jesus thank you for dying on the cross to redeem me from my sins. Please forgive the sins I've committed (both knowingly and unknowingly) and I ask that you heal all the wounds in my soul. Please forgive the sins of my generational line and all past sins passed down through the generations. I repent of all sin, transgressions, iniquity and humble myself and my bloodline under your mighty hand. I believe you wash me clean, heal me of all trauma I've experienced and cleanse all soul wounds in my blood line. I believe you love me unconditionally and cause me to breakthrough. I thank you and praise you in advance for victory. In Jesus name amen!

Stress

As pressure and stress bear down on me, I find joy in your commands.

Psalm 119:143

Stress exhibits itself in many and causes our health to be affected, which in turn affects our soul and spirit. Living in a constant state of stress, flight or fight, puts our adrenal system and organs in an unnatural state. If you have been feeling exhausted, beat down, ineffective, moody and exhibit heath problems; perhaps all the worrying and stress has caused it. It can make you question your sanity when your body is a mess!

We have developed the habit of reacting instead of responding to life's daily issues and become very sensitive when our body is in a state of stress. We are like pincushions easily offended, hurt and upset. If you have seen the kids movie "Chicken Little" you will remember how he would look at the sky and in a dramatic move start flapping about saying "The sky is falling! The sky is falling!" If you feel a like Chicken Little and the sky seems to be falling in your world on a daily basis, perhaps it might not be a spiritual issue but a physical one. Most of us living in the 21st century have become so accustomed to living in a constant state of stress, we hardly recognize it as abnormal. It has become so normal that everyone seems to be "busy" and stressed these days, it is like a badge of honour!

A recent visit to the doctor made me acutely aware of this phenomenon. Contrary to my own belief, I thought my persistent state of hyper awareness and high metabolism was a good thing, until she pointed something out. She explained that my body was at risk of more serious health issues if I did not address the symptoms and causes of my stress. My heart palpitations, moodiness, tiredness, eye twitching, and lack of appetite were symptoms that my organs were living in a constant state of adrenalin.

Ask any medical doctor or a simple Google search will spit out a laundry list of adverse symptoms of a body under stress. According to the American Institute of Stress **(19)** 77% of people regularly experience physical symptoms caused by stress, and **(20)** 75-90% of visits to a primary care doctor is a result from stress related disorders. Granted, there are times when stress is a good thing; like when you have a deadline and you need to hyper focus, or when a hungry lion is stalking you in the African bush and you have to run for your life! These instances should be the exception not the rule.

Even though we know it is not good for us, we do not know how to live in any other way. It is become the way we "see" life. Think of it as a when you get your eyes checked at the eye doctor. You have been walking around happily seeing the world in your own way, until the test reveals your eyesight is not 20/20. The optometrist hands you a new set of eyeglasses and suddenly the details are crisp, the colours more vibrant and you can finally see! Once you have seen it you cannot "unsee" it, and now this new technicolour view on life is your new normal. We need to approach dealing with stress in the same way. Do not just accept it as your normal, have your 'eyes tested' and get a reality check. Was that meltdown you had by freaking out at your child because of them or was it that you are just over tired and freak out is your middle name?

Thankfully with God's help we can identity the root causes of our stress and ask Him to help us through it. Of course there is no easy immediate fix, but simply being aware of how we react vs how we respond can help us manage our stress a little better. Asking the Holy Spirit to remind us when we are getting close to boiling point can help us avoid going nuclear. That inkling that says "it's time to put your phone down and go to bed" is very practical advice that the Holy Spirit is very happy to offer. So do not forget what mama used to say about getting a good night's rest and everything will look better in the morning....

Prayer: Release from Stress

Dear Lord thank You for caring so much for me that you want me to be well. I repent for allowing stress to affect my mind, body and soul. Please forgive my acts of disobedience and for not listening to your warnings. I release the healing power of dunamis to flood every cell in my body and repair all damage in Jesus name amen!

Your MISSION, should you choose to accept it, is to suit up and do the boot camp training, put on those big girl panties and get to work shattering the kingdom of darkness!

4. Barriers in The Mind

Negative Thoughts

We destroy arguments and every lofty opinion raised against the knowledge of God, and take every thought captive to obey Christ.

2 Corinthians 10:5

It is so important that we start each day with good thinking habits. Making sure we cover our minds with the armour of God before our feet hit the floor in the morning is how you start our day right. We do not want to keep ourselves stuck in despair, and prevent our blessings from flowing, so it is imperative that we take each thought captive. We do not want our stinking thinking to become a runaway train, in fact we should not allow the negative train to leave the station!

It is our job to choose to stop the thought as soon as it appears. The Holy Spirit is our helper and will gently remind you when a thought has been sent by the enemy. For example, when we are bombarded with a spirit of fear that brings the feeling of dread, we revoke access by sending the spirit back to the pit. We speak the truth, which is God's Word, so in this case you would say "God has not given me a spirit of fear but of power, love and a sound mind. You spirit of fear be gone in Jesus name!" (2 Timothy 1:7). The spirit will have no choice but to vacate immediately. That is how we take every thought captive to make it obedient to Christ.

When in doubt, repent. Repentance brings us back into alignment with God and revokes any access the enemy might have over your mind, body and soul. Every word and every action starts with a thought so it is very important to train our thoughts to be God's thoughts.

Isaiah 55:8

For my thoughts are not your thoughts, neither are your ways my ways,"
declares the LORD.

See also Matthew 9:4, Matthew 15:19, Job 20:2, Isaiah 55:9, Romans 2:15.

Prayer: Release from Negative Thoughts

Dear Lord I thank you for the redeeming power of Jesus who died and was raised from the dead for me. I repent for dwelling on any negative, evil, wrong thoughts and bring my mind into obedience to Christ. I seal up any access points that my thoughts have given to the enemy and I seal my mind with the blood of Jesus and wear the helmet of salvation. Thank you for saving me in Jesus name amen!

Rejection

You are coming to Christ, who is the living cornerstone of God's temple.
He was rejected by people, but he was chosen by God for great honor.

1 Peter 2:4

Do you remember a time in your life when you were made to feel less than, stupid, irrelevant, not good enough, invisible, ignored, rejected? It is a painful experience when you feel like your heart is being ripped into pieces with the stabbing wounds of the arrows of rejection. It can leave lasting consequences if left unchecked. For many years I was a walking pincushion of rejection. Every time I was ignored, excluded, told to shut up, or made to feel my opinion did not matter; a wound of rejection would take hold. The wounds go so far back I cannot remember the first time it happened. It is as if it became part of my personality and I just learnt to accept it. One thing I do remember is making a promise to myself; "One day I will show them, I am not going to let anyone ever make me feel like that again." It skewed my goals and ambitions as everything was tainted with rejection where my motivation was to prove to everyone that I did matter, that I am clever, and that I have value. It became the glasses that I viewed life and relationships, and caused me to pursue approval from others just so I could love myself. I will admit it I am a recovered people pleaser who was formerly addicted to approval!

Rejection is the root of a lot of problems. It is one of those insidious roots that gives rise to many rotten branches. Left unchecked the roots of rejection grow into bitterness, then indifference, hatred, witchcraft, and eventually death or suicide. There are millions of people walking around today with wounds from rejection that have altered their decisions, mindsets, occupations, locations and relationships. When we are hurt from rejection we will do whatever it takes to avoid feeling that way again. When you feel like you are not good enough, are misunderstood, and excluded from social groups, it only exasperates the deep seated emotion. Rejection breeds rejection and once we are wounded with its poison arrow it warps our perception of people, conversations and outcomes. Eventually we can only view things from a rejection point of view where everyone seems to reject us and we are hurt by the smallest things. Our reaction from rejection causes loneliness, misery, self-pity, depression, despair, and death or suicide.

Proverbs 18:14

The human spirit can endure in sickness, but a crushed spirit who can bear?

It does not take much to be stung with rejection, often it starts in childhood or as far back as the womb. Rejection can start from conception when a mother has a surprise pregnancy and a sense of being unwanted is passed onto the baby. Rejection can start when a child is not shown love, feels less favoured by its parents, or experiences a traumatic event. Rejection is an inner attitude or propensity of thinking, and is a demonic spirit that enters through hurt emotions. These wounds may not be known by our mind, reason or memory. They develop in the dark and hide in our soul as wounds. Derek Prince **(1)** says "Rejection, very frequently, is in that deep area in the spirit. And often, because it's so deep, people do not even realize their problem is rejection." Our spirit knows exactly what is in our mind and soul and so we need to dig deep with the help of the Holy Spirit to unearth the roots of rejection. There are two pendulum sides to rejection: passive (self-loathing, worthless, low self esteem) or aggressive (selfish ambition, perfectionism, people pleasing, high achiever, independence). These fruits are symptoms of the root of rejection. The progressions starts with feeling hurt, then hardness or heart, indifference, then rebellion and witchcraft.

1 Samuel 15:23

For rebellion is like the sin of divination, and arrogance like the evil of idolatry. Because you have rejected the word of the LORD, he has rejected you as king.

To move from rejection to acceptance we need to rely on the Word of God which is based on facts not feelings. The fact is that Christ died for us, He was buried and He rose again on the third day. As believers our faith is built on believing the gospel that what Christ did was enough for us to live in victory. We act on facts and our feelings will follow our faith. It is a decision, not based on whether or not we "feel" good or bad about ourselves. Jesus paid the ultimate price and was rejected for us;

Isaiah 53:3

He was despised and rejected by mankind, a man of suffering, and familiar with pain. Like one from whom people hide their faces he was despised, and we held him in low esteem.

Knowing that Jesus made the ultimate sacrifice, we can accept our healing and activate acceptance. How we move past rejection into Christ's acceptance is by starting with forgiveness. Forgiveness is the key that unlocks all doors of the dungeon of your soul that have held you in prison to fear, isolation and defeat. We need to lay down any bitterness, resentment, rebellion and hatred we are harboring in our hearts. Remember it is a choice, not a feeling irrespective of how badly you were hurt. Next we have to rely on the facts that we are accepted by Christ. Lastly you need to accept yourself, never speak badly about yourself or agree with the harassment of the enemy. Keep declaring you are a child of God who is loved and favoured, and eventually your feelings will catch up with the choice you have made.

Prayer: Release from Rejection

Dear Lord thank You for sending your Son to die for me and for taking on rejection so that I don't have be rejected. I ask for your forgiveness for harboring bitterness, resentment, rebellion and hatred in my heart toward _____ (insert name/s). I break off all traces of the root of rejection from my mind, heart, body and soul. I repent for agreeing with the enemy and cancel all negative words I've spoken over myself. I receive your love and acceptance through Christ Jesus. I declare and decree I am a child of God who is loved and accepted unconditionally. Thank you for my healing in Jesus name amen!

Pride

Pride goes before destruction, and haughtiness before a fall.

Proverbs 16:18

Pride is often an instigator for a lot of issues, especially things like resentment and anger. Pride in Proverbs 16:18 clearly says "Pride comes before a fall,". What this means is while we think we are so fabulous, we are blinded by our own weaknesses. The big problem with pride is that proud people often will not admit they suffer from it and therein lies the problem. It takes a lot for us to admit we need to be delivered from a spirit of pride. For many years I refused to admit I had a problem with pride. It was a defense mechanism from keeping my feelings from getting hurt from my past experiences with rejection. When left to fester it grows like a stubborn tree than needs a pickaxe to dig out.

Why do you judge the speck in your brothers eye when you have a plank in your own? I know it sounds cliché, but if you are so worried about what your brother or sister in Christ is doing and you like to criticize them, maybe we need to look within first. Have you considered that perhaps you might be the one in the wrong? Is what you are criticizing in them something that you are struggling with yourself? Pride holds up a mirror to our own failings. Ouch! If that stings and makes you feel uncomfortable, annoyed or angry; then we have definitely hit a nerve. It means that it is an issue in you that needs to be dealt with.

The devil loves to use pride because if we look in the scriptures, pride is what caused him to fall. He was a beautiful creature created by God for God's good pleasure, and yet pride got hold of him. He thought he was better than God and because of his pride he got ousted out of Heaven. He lost out on all the blessings that God had for him. Are you harsh, hard, judgmental, critical, easily annoyed and angered? These are classic signs or fruit that there is a root of pride brewing underground.

Proverbs 11:2

Pride leads to disgrace, but with humility comes wisdom.

Some notable scriptures on pride are Proverbs 8:13, Proverbs 13:10, Proverbs 29:23, James 4 : 1-6, Romans 12:3, Ephesian 4:26, Proverbs 3:34, James 4:6.

Pride comes in different forms like national pride and personal pride. Pride is known to ruin relationships, especially between a husband and wife. Personal pride can be a sign that we are blinded by the truth. During arguments do you find yourself clinging to your pride? If so that can make reconciling your differences a whole lot harder. Being willing to be humble requires us to swallow our pride and step away from our burning desire to be right. We need to step out of our sense of self-justification and hurt for the greater good of our relationships. If your pride drives you to win every argument and you refuse to apologize for your mistakes, you may find yourself stuck in the mud of anger, resentment and eventually hatred. To insist upon our own way puts us on the path toward destruction because it illustrates our urge to be independent of God. The dangerous thing is that God will put you in a situation where you will have no way out but to humble yourself. Have you had an argument with someone and you are left with this icky, burning sensation in your chest? Have you given the person the cold shoulder, ignored their calls and texts, and sulked for days? Did they not meet your expectations for something and now you are ticked?

Ecclesiastes 7:9

Do not be quickly provoked in your spirit, for anger resides in the lap of fools.

The Holy Spirit within you will burn with uncomfortable fervor until you resolve the issue and let go of pride, anger and resentment. Going to sleep whilst you are still angry will only exasperate your problem until you repent of your sin of anger and pride. This is especially true with married couples. For example, she gets upset with him because he forgot to give her a gift she was expecting for a birthday or anniversary. Now she is giving him the cold shoulder, refusing to make him food or spend time with him. The poor dude probably does not know why he is in the dog box!

Do yourself a favour and forgive, repent and cast out the spirit of pride. Today pride is often one of those unspoken failings that Satan likes to deceive us with because he has a sneaky way of making us think that we do not have a problem of pride when we actually do. It is the humble that are able to say, "I've been prideful, I've been wrong. God show me the way." So, if you are reading this and you think you do not have a problem with pride, perhaps I would suggest we pray and let God reveal to you if there has been any root of pride so you can get rid of it immediately. God's remedy for pride is to submit ourselves in humility.

1 Peter 5:5-6 New King James Version (NKJV)

5 Likewise you younger people, submit yourselves to your elders. Yes, all of you be submissive to one another, and be clothed with humility, for "God resists the proud, But gives grace to the humble." 6 Therefore humble yourselves under the mighty hand of God, that He may exalt you in due time.

Prayer: Release from Pride

Dear Lord Jesus, please forgive me for allowing pride in my life. I humble myself before you as I choose humility over pride. I confess that I have insisted on having my own way and clinging to pride. I ask for your forgiveness. Thank you for revealing to me where the roots of pride so that I can make amends. With the situation of _____ (insert conflict) that you have brought to my mind where pride has been a barrier, as an act of my will I yield myself to you and release the pride that has held me captive. I choose to step away from pride, I humble myself and ask for their forgiveness. God I need your help and grace. I break off the spirit of pride and loose its hold on me in Jesus name. Thank you God for your unconditional love and for my healing, in Jesus name amen!

A good exercise is to go to the individuals you have hurt or argued with and ask for forgiveness as a step toward humbling yourself and activating your healing.

Anger

Get rid of all bitterness, rage, anger, harsh words, and slander, as well as all types of evil behaviour.

Ephesians 4:31

How do you behave behind the wheel of your car? Do you lose your tonsils when you are cut off in traffic? Does sitting in bumper to bumper traffic make you boil? How we react when we are sitting behind the wheel of our car is a good indication on the health of our souls as it puts us in a position we cannot control. Anger is a physical symptom of an inward condition. Anger fuels our adrenaline, lowers our immune system and hijacks our thinking.

Colossians 3:8

But now you must also rid yourselves of all such things as these: anger, rage, malice, slander, and filthy language from your lips.

Anger **(2)** is an emotion we experience in our body as well as our mind. The physiological events that occur when we get angry are complex, starting with the amygdala in our brains. It is those almond shaped structures that set off our fight or flight response and flood our body with chemicals. The amygdalas purpose is to warn us about possible threats and puts our body into immediate action to protect us from danger. Our brain is wired to cause us to act before we get a chance to assess whether we are in fact in real imminent danger. During a fit of anger the neurotransmitters in your brain triggers a series of events from increasing your heart rate, muscles tense, boosting your blood pressure, increased breathing, increased blood flow, focused attention, and adrenaline and noradrenaline flood your system. Part of our brain literally shuts off when we get angry. The term "blind rage" is true because your brain switches off your reasoning and you lock focus on the cause of your anger. Now you are ready to fight! Once the perceived threat is over our body calms down back to it is resting state but it is difficult to relax. The effects of adrenalin flowing through our veins can make us susceptible to getting angry again. This means that the smallest things can set us off and the angry cycle starts all over again. During these fits we find it difficult to remember details and it decreases our ability to concentrate. Did you have a parent, spouse or a friend who would get angry and then deny their fault in the argument the next day? This explains a lot.

Studies show **(3)** that the effects of a constant flood of stress chemicals that unmanaged anger causes can eventually cause harm to different systems of the body. Some of the short and long-term health problems that have been related to anger include: headaches, digestion problems, abdominal pain, insomnia, anxiety, depression, high blood pressure, skin problems, heart attack, and stroke. Besides the physiological effects on the body, anger affects our soul and spirit too. Anger opens us up to demonic influence. When we lose our temper in a fit of rage we lose control over our reasoning and decision making abilities making us open to other influences. We could argue that our brain is wired to react in anger instinctually but learning to manage our anger is a skill we can learn. The concept of "anger management" is true.

The Greek word for "provoke" is paroxusmos **(4)** which means "stimulation, provocation, irritation, angry dispute". Provoke is the same word from which the English word paroxysm is derived. A paroxysm **(5)** is a fit, attack, or sudden increase or recurrence of symptoms (as of a disease), convulsion, a sudden violent emotion or action, an outburst a paroxysm of rage, a paroxysm of laughter.

Ephesians 4:31

Get rid of all bitterness, rage and anger, brawling and slander, along with every form of malice.

The good news is that where anger destroys, God can forgive us and heal all affected areas of our body, spirit and soul.

Proverbs 15:1

A gentle answer turns away wrath, but a harsh word stirs up anger.

This scripture shows us that the words we use can either stir up anger or turn wrath away. Our mouth gets us in trouble a lot! If we can recognize what triggers us and pray for God's peace to flow through us, we can manage our anger God's way.

Prayer: Release from Anger

Dear Lord thank you for your grace and mercy. I ask for forgiveness for my angry outbursts and losing control. I repent of the harsh, hard, pressing and destructive words I have used in a fit of rage. Please cleanse me of all unrighteousness and seal up any open doors I have opened to the enemy by sinning by getting angry. I break off the spirit of anger in me and in my bloodline in Jesus name. I cancel all effects and break any curses that have had power over me and my family. Thank you Lord that you are healing every area of my body, spirit and soul. I release the resurrection dunamis power in me in Jesus name amen!

Once you've repented and reconciled yourself to God, you can make your healing complete by asking for forgiveness from those you have hurt or wronged during your angry outbursts. Apologizing goes a long way to reconciling relationships destroyed by the spirit of anger.

Bitterness

Another dies in bitterness of soul, never having enjoyed anything good.

Job 21:25

Bitterness is another insidious symptom that goes along with rejection, jealousy and fear. The saying it is a "bitter pill to swallow" **(6)** refers to something that is very unpleasant but must be accepted, such as losing to a younger player in a game. A bitter person gets delight from seeing others fail when the other person's failure makes them feel better about themselves.

Bitterness **(7)** shows up as shame (Proverbs 12:4), reproach which is an expression of rebuke or disapproval **(8)** (Psalm 42:10), cursing (Psalm 109:18), unconfessed sin (Psalm 32:3), envy (Proverbs 14:30), a broken spirit (Proverbs 17:22), trouble in life (Psalm 102:3), fever and disease (Job 30:30), fear and shaking (Job 4:14), captivity to sin (Acts 8:23), early aging (Job 20:11), agony and distress from God's chastening (Psalm 6:2, Job 33:19), suffering and affliction of the soul (Job 30:16), restlessness (Job 30:17), iniquity (Ezekiel 32:27), grief (Psalm 31:10), curse of sin (Psalm 22:14).

Did you know that your body will show physical signs that you harbor bitterness in your soul? Bitterness of soul rots the bones. Healthy bones are a sign of good health, and unhealthy bones are a sign of poor health. Bones are where the body manufactures the blood which is the life line of our body. Bitterness dries up the bones and causes serious illness and possibly death.

Our bones are where bone marrow is formed. Marrow is important to sustaining life and manages our immune system which helps us ward off disease. According to Medical News Today **(9)**;

"Bone marrow is the spongy tissue inside some of the bones in the body, including the hip and thigh bones. Healthy bone marrow and blood cells are needed in order to live. Bone marrow contains immature cells, called stem cells. Many people with blood, cancers, leukemia, sickle cell anemia, and other life-threatening diseases, rely on bone marrow or cord blood transplants to survive. Bone marrow produces 200 billion new red blood cells every day, along with white blood cells and platelets. Bone marrow contains mesenchymal and hematopoietic stem cells. Around 10,000 people in the US are diagnosed each year with diseases that require bone marrow transplants. Several diseases pose a threat to bone marrow and prevent bone marrow from turning stem cells into essential cells. When disease affects bone marrow so that it can no longer function effectively, a marrow or cord blood transplant could be the best treatment option; for some patients it is the only potential cure."

Leviticus 17:11

For the life of a creature is in the blood, and I have given it to you to make atonement for yourselves on the altar; it is the blood that makes atonement for one's life.

God's Word is clear about the dangers of allowing bitterness to grow in our spirit, soul and body; Romans 3:14, Job 7:11, Acts 8:23, Hebrews 12:, Ephesians 4:31-32, Proverbs 14:10.

In Old Testament times there was a test for an unfaithful wife that used bitter water as a tool. If a husband suspected that his wife was unfaithful he would take her to the priest who would make her drink holy water where she would speak a curse upon herself. If she was innocent nothing would happen to her, but if she was guilty her belly would bloat, she would become sterile, she would endure bitter suffering and thigh rot. How awful!

Numbers 5:12-28

12 "Speak to the Israelites and say to them: 'If a man's wife goes astray and is unfaithful to him 13 so that another man has sexual relations with her, and this is hidden from her husband and her impurity is undetected (since there is no witness against her and she has not been caught in the act), 14 and if feelings of jealousy come over her husband and he suspects his wife and she is impure—or if he is jealous and suspects her even though she is not impure— 15 then he is to take his wife to the priest. He must also take an offering of a tenth of an ephah of barley flour on her behalf. He must not pour olive oil on it or put incense on it, because it is a grain offering for jealousy, a reminder offering to draw attention to wrongdoing. 16 "'The priest shall bring her and have her stand before the Lord. 17 Then he shall take some holy water in a clay jar and put some dust from the tabernacle floor into the water. 18 After the priest has had the woman stand before the Lord, he shall loosen her hair and place in her hands the reminder-offering, the grain offering for jealousy, while he himself holds the bitter water that brings a curse. 19 Then the priest shall put the woman under oath and say to her, "If no other man has had sexual relations with you and you have not gone astray and become impure while married to your husband, may this bitter water that brings a curse not harm you. 20 But if you have gone astray while married to your husband and you have made yourself impure by having sexual relations with a man other than your husband", 21 here the priest is to put the woman under this curse – "may the Lord cause you to become a curse among your people when he makes your womb miscarry and your abdomen swell. 22 May this water that brings a curse enter your body so that your abdomen swells or your womb miscarries." "'Then the woman is to say, "Amen. So be it." 23 "'The priest is to write these curses on a scroll and then wash them off into the bitter water. 24 He shall make the woman drink the bitter water that brings a curse, and this water that brings a curse and causes bitter suffering will enter her. 25 The priest is to take from her hands the grain offering for jealousy, wave it before the Lord and bring it to the altar. 26 The priest is then to take a handful of the grain offering as a memorial offering and burn it on the altar; after that, he is to have the woman drink the water. 27 If she has made herself impure and been unfaithful to her husband, this will be the result: When she is made to

drink the water that brings a curse and causes bitter suffering, it will enter her, her abdomen will swell and her womb will miscarry, and she will become a curse. 28 If, however, the woman has not made herself impure, but is clean, she will be cleared of guilt and will be able to have children.

The New King James version says in verse 22;

22 and may this water that causes the curse go into your stomach, and make your belly swell and your thigh rot."

Pretty scary stuff! This is a vivid example that bitterness can cause our belly to bloat with inflammation, cause suffering, and make a person infertile. Of course we do not live under the laws of the Old Testament because Jesus came to redeem us, but the laws of cause and effect still count. Have you found yourself speaking words of bitterness, anger, jealousy, criticism and hatred toward someone? If you found your body retaining water, your abdomen swelling and you feel generally unwell; it could be a sign that you have "drunk of the bitter water". We are body, spirit and soul and you cannot separate one from the other. Do not be surprised if your body reacts to a spike in your blood pressure when you go nuclear losing your temper, or you feel unwell when you curse someone who has offended or hurt you. Anger and bitterness go together. Angry, critical wounds cause stress on our bodies and water retention. Our body is constantly trying to heal itself and swelling is a sign of distress and inflammation. The remedy is forgiveness, forgive quickly and often and receive God's healing to your body, spirit and soul.

Ephesian 4:31

Get rid of all bitterness, rage and anger, brawling and slander, along with every form of malice.

Prayer: Release from Bitterness

Dear Lord thank you for the redeeming power of Jesus's sacrifice on the cross. I ask for forgiveness for the words and thoughts of bitterness I have allowed in my life. I repent of my sin of bitterness. Please wash me with the blood of Jesus and cleanse me of any disease in my bones, my blood and my body that is a result of bitterness. I cancel all negative and destructive words of bitterness I have spoken over myself and others. I close all doors to the enemy that were opened due to my sin of bitterness and seal my mind, body and soul with the blood of Jesus. I receive your healing now in Jesus name amen!

Perfectionism

As it is written: "There is no one righteous, not even one."

Romans 3:10

A common symptom of rejection is perfectionism. Feeling like you are not good enough unless it is done perfect is typical of the root of rejection that has buried itself in our soul. For years I had to be perfect and any time I fell short of perfect (which was all the time) I would beat myself up, talk to myself badly and give myself a "stern talking to". The fruit of perfectionism is often caused by high expectations that were placed on us as children by our parents, our teachers and peers. It can also be the result of rejection where we have been made to feel less lovable if our behaviour did not measure up. Often times we are our own worst critic and we are harder on ourselves than we would be on anyone else. Someone who suffers from perfectionism is often a workaholic who does not know how to stop and smell the roses because they are always chasing the next thing. Perfectionism also creates physical symptoms like stress, depression and eating disorders **(10)**. Striving for perfect is like chasing a mirage. As soon as you think you have reached perfection, the goal posts change and it is beyond your reach. No one is perfect except God. As Christians our goal should be to develop a heart that is perfect toward God. What this means is that it is not based on our works or behaviour, but on the condition of our heart which shows our motives.

James 3:2

We all stumble in many ways. Anyone who is never at fault in what they say is perfect, able to keep their whole body in check.

Derek Prince says **(11)** the Spirit of the Lord is always looking to find a certain type of person whose heart is perfect toward God. We see this in the life of Abraham (Genesis 17:1) and Job (Job 1:8), both men were totally sold out to God and followed God's leading in their lives and God did miraculous things through them due to their obedience. God searches our hearts, intentions and motives and knows us better than we know ourselves. We might be able to fool others but God knows the ultimate health of our heart.

Luke 16:15

15 And he said to them, "You are those who justify yourselves before men, but God knows your hearts. For what is exalted among men is an abomination in the sight of God."

Perfection toward God is about having a right heart attitude toward God, and a right attitude toward evil. There is no compromise with God, you are absolutely committed to being obedient no matter what it costs. Are you ready to be fully committed to God? The good news is that we do not have to do anything in our own strength because we rely on Jesus to make us perfect, it is just up to us to choose.

Philippians 3 :12-14

12 Not that I have already obtained this or am already perfect, but I press on to make it my own, because Christ Jesus has made me his own. 13 Brothers, I do not consider that I have made it my own. But one thing I do: forgetting what lies behind and straining forward to what lies ahead, 14 I press on toward the goal for the prize of the upward call of God in Christ Jesus.

Prayer: Release from Perfectionism

Dear Lord thank you for the redeeming power of your son Jesus and that His death and resurrection makes me perfect in your eyes. I repent for allowing the negative spirit of perfectionism to run my thoughts, words, and actions. I ask for you to search my heart God and clear out all destructive patterns, habits and mindsets. Make my heart new and perfect toward You. I choose to do Your will in my life and come into obedience under your Word. Thank you for healing me in Jesus name amen!

Rebellion

Rebellion is as sinful as witchcraft, and stubbornness as bad as worshiping idols. So because you have rejected the command of the LORD, he has rejected you as king.

1 Samuel 15:23

Unresolved rebellion is the root of many ills. Rebellion is a common sin amongst all of humanity. Whether it was the Industrial Revolution or the hippie movement of the 60's, rebellion has been at the root of many hostile takeovers and over throws. The modern take of "Rebel without a Cause" is someone who is the troubled underdog who fights against authority and is perceived to be cool. However, the problem with rebellion is that it is stepping outside of God's protection. When we go against authority it brings judgement upon ourselves. The scariest part of rebellion is that it can cause harm to our children and future generations.

Romans 13:2

Consequently, whoever rebels against the authority is rebelling against what God has instituted, and those who do so will bring judgment on themselves.

Numbers 14:18

The LORD is slow to anger and filled with unfailing love, forgiving every kind of sin and rebellion. But he does not excuse the guilty. He lays the sins of the parents upon their children; the entire family is affected–even children in the third and fourth generations.

Have you noticed that relationships that were started in rebellion never seem to last? For example, when there is adultery and the mistress becomes the wife, usually about ten years later the couple split and the saga continues. Anyone remember the drama around Brad Pitt, Jennifer Aniston and Angelina Jolie? Do you know of someone who ran away from home with their lover against the advice of their parents, only to find themselves divorced years later? Even though we may disagree with the choices that our authority figures make (aka our President, government, parent, teacher, spouse or employer), God is clear that we are to be respectful of their authority because God is ultimately in control. If you have found yourself criticizing your President or government because you disagree with his/her policies, or your boss because you disagree with his management skills, that is also cause for rebellion.

If you have found that your blessings have dried up, your prayers are not being answered and there is havoc in your home; consider if you have been disobedient or rebellious to God's promptings. What is the last thing God told you to do? Have you been resisting, procrastinating or refusing to do what He has told you to do? Even though it might be hard, inconvenient, or embarrassing you need to obey before God will release you to move onto the next thing. I personally found this to be true when I heard the Holy Spirit telling me to do something, then when I tried to ignore it my prayers fell on deaf ears and I was stuck. After praying really hard I heard the words "you need to do the last thing I told you to do". That was not the easy answer I was looking for because I knew the instruction would mean taking a step toward something that scared me.

Another side of rebellion is doing something that is in direct contrast to God's Word. Perhaps you find yourself living in sin with someone whom you are not married to, and you try to convince yourself that it is okay because you love him and hope your Christian behaviour will turn him to God. Let me tell you honey, two wrongs do not make a right because God is clear about sin and rebellion;

Galatians 5: 16-21

16 So I say, walk by the Spirit, and you will not gratify the desires of the flesh. 17 For the flesh desires what is contrary to the Spirit, and the Spirit what is contrary to the flesh. They are in conflict with each other, so that you are not to do whatever you want. 18 But if you are led by the Spirit, you are not under the law. 19 The acts of the flesh are obvious: sexual immorality, impurity and debauchery; 20 idolatry and witchcraft; hatred, discord, jealousy, fits of rage, selfish ambition, dissensions, factions 21 and envy; drunkenness, orgies, and the like. I warn you, as I did before, that those who live like this will not inherit the kingdom of God.

The dangerous problem with rebellion is that it is more than an attitude or a heart problem, it is likened to witchcraft. Witchcraft brings curses right down to the fourth generation. God does not give us commands and instructions to be mean or to ruin our fun, He does it because He loves us and knows what is good for us. Just like any good parent He knows the consequences of sin can ruin your life, delay your future and create repercussions that will permanently alter your life. Rebellion causes us to sin and we will not inherit the Kingdom of heaven if we refuse to repent.

The good news is that we have a divine exchange through Jesus. He took on all the evil our rebellion deserved so that all the good that Jesus is (because of his perfect obedience), forgiveness would be offered to us in exchange. Jesus took our punishment that we rightfully deserved. What a sweet deal!

Prayer: Release from Rebellion

Dear Lord thank you for Jesus and the work of the Cross. I declare that I have received life because Jesus was willing to die for me. I repent of all my sins of rebellion and witchcraft against my authority figures _____ (insert names). I now come to obedience in Christ Jesus. I break off, bind and cancel the curses in my generational line that are due to disobedience, rebellion and witchcraft from the acts of my ancestors right back to Adam. I receive your forgiveness of sins, grace and mercy for me and my family. In Jesus name amen!

Reasoning

When I was a child, I spoke and thought and reasoned as a child. But when I grew up, I put away childish things.

1 Corinthians 13:11

As a child I would often annoy and frustrate my parents because I constantly asked "But why?". My mind was always asking questions trying to figure out the world. When there would be no good answer (or my mother was too tired to explain it) she would say "Because Y is a crooked letter that can't be straightened". She would then get my classic eye roll. This habit persisted and now as an adult I still find myself reasoning, trying to figure out the answers to some impossible questions. Reasoning and worry go together. Excessive reasoning keeps us imagining every conceivable result, and often we end up anxious and stressed. Overactive reasoning takes us away from discernment of the heart, and a wavering mind keeps us in indecision.

Ephesians 4:14

Then we will no longer be infants, tossed back and forth by the waves, and blown here and there by every wind of teaching and by the cunning and craftiness of people in their deceitful scheming.

Excessive reasoning indicates a lack of trust in God. Questioning everything until we feel we have a justifiable answer will prevent progress. Was that God who spoke to me? What if I make the wrong decision? How do I know if that is really God? Why God do you want me to do that? God is clear that we are not to be double minded.

It is the same with raising children, we get annoyed when our kids do not listen when we give an instruction and talk back. Sometimes we do not have to give a reason because as parents we have sound judgement and can see the pitfalls up ahead. It is the same with God, we should obey without arguing or reasoning. God expects obedience from His children and prefers it to sacrifice.

1 Samuel 15:22

But Samuel replied: "Does the LORD delight in burnt offerings and sacrifices as much as in obeying the LORD? To obey is better than sacrifice, and to heed is better than the fat of rams.

How can we tell if what we are hearing is in fact the voice of God? The enemy likes to mimic the tone of our voice and twist the sound of Gods, but we have a tool for authenticity. The voice of God comes through the Holy Spirit who lives in our spirit. He is pure, peaceful, obedient, merciful, kind and sincere. If the instruction you are hearing follows these guidelines and lines up with the Word of God, you know it is genuine. The enemy has no good in him so he would rather stick a finger in his own eye than be kind, merciful or peaceful. If you sense the voice is harassing, hard, and pressing and sounds like this; "What you gonna do? What you gonna do? Are you weak? You cannot sit back and do nothing!" that sounds like someone evil has hijacked the airways.

How do we tell if we have blockages to hearing God's voice? Often times it can be a result of barriers (just like we have covered in this chapter), and especially disobedience. If God gives us an instruction and we disobey, His voice gets softer and softer until He seems far away. He will not give you a new instruction until you have obeyed the last thing He told you to do. If you feel far from God seek Him first by studying the Word on the subject. Ask God to reveal to you the last thing He told you to do that you may have ignored or dismissed.

1 John 1:6

If we claim to have fellowship with him and yet walk in the darkness, we lie and do not live out the truth.

The Word in the Bible is the ultimate authority we have to live by. It is alive and active, and will speak to you right where you at no matter your season in life. It is sharper than any sword and will cut through the noise and confusion with clarity. It will tell us the truth even when we do not want to hear it, and that convicting feeling we get from the Holy Spirit when we read it is confirmation of its truth.

Hebrews 4:12

For the word of God is alive and active. Sharper than any double-edged sword, it penetrates even to dividing soul and spirit, joints and marrow; it judges the thoughts and attitudes of the heart.

If you still find yourself struggling to accept the truth and you still feel uncertain, check your peace. When we are walking in faith and trusting God to work all things out for our good, our peace will calm our mind and soul. However, we must seek God with intent and have confidence that He will answer us when we genuinely seek Him for an answer.

Hebrews 11:6

And without faith it is impossible to please God, because anyone who comes to him must believe that he exists and that he rewards those who earnestly seek him.

This means you do not ask God then think "Yeah well, I bet I won't get an answer because I never do." Stop. Look. Listen. Arrest that thought and speak God's Word out loud so your brain will hear what you know in your heart to be true.

Prayer: Release from Excessive Reasoning

Dear Lord thank you for giving me the Holy Spirit as my comforter and friend. I repent of excessive reasoning, of relying on my own strength and abilities, and for disobeying your instructions. Please forgive my lack of faith. I declare my mind is set on the will of God and I trust You to work all things out for my good. Lord please remove all mental blockages that are hindering me hearing your voice clearly. Thank you for delivering me in Jesus name amen!

5. Barriers in Moods

Fear

There is no fear in love, but perfect love casts out fear. For fear has to do with punishment, and whoever fears has not been perfected in love.

1 John 4:18

Ever had one of those days where the voices in your head are harassing you with words like: "You cannot do this, what if you fail, what will they think of you, what if you get hurt, nobody cares about you, it is no use in even trying, you may as well give up now, why bother it is a waste of your time, it won't last, you are too old, you are too young, it will never end, you look ugly, nobody will ever love you, who do you think you are..."

The list of belligerent harassing words never seem to cease. The record player gets stuck in this perpetual cycle of downers that feels like you will never see the sunshine. Let me tell you my darling that fear is a liar! It gets you thinking that those words are just your thoughts and bullies you into giving up on yourself and your dreams. The sneaky thing is that fear sounds awfully like your own voice, it is a seasoned thespian who can mimic your moods, your voice and your tone. But, and this is a big but, he is not the real you! He is busy masquerading around your head making you think you are going crazy, because his sleeze ball techniques are so slimy he knows if he tries long enough he will get you defeated. Yes I will say it again the sound of fear is NOT the real you!

Some of the symptoms of fear include: anxiousness, racing heart rate, sweaty palms, low self esteem, inactivity, lack of energy, feelings of depression, sadness, lack of peace, short temper, loss of joy etc. As you can see many of the symptoms involve immobilizing you into inaction so that you cannot be effective using your gifts and talents. We do need to keep in mind there are times when fear can be a good thing, like when your life is in danger and you need to flee or fight for your life. Those instances are very few and far between. So the constant feeling of fear we experience on a daily basis is not necessary nor effective.

The first thing we need to realize about that punk loser is that it is a demonic spirit, it is not your own thoughts and it is not acceptable. Just think of it this way, would you allow someone to talk to you out loud like that, or to someone you love? I did not think so... Fear is a liar, a bully and a thief and he is part of that punk gang from down under who all have the same agenda: steal, kill, destroy. Ugh it makes me angry! However the good news is that we are onto him! We know his punk like tactics and we are going to destroy them once and for all!

2 Timothy 1:7 says in the New International version;

For the Spirit God gave us does not make us timid, but gives us power, love and self-discipline.

The spirit of fear is described as 'timid' and 'cowardly'. The promise in God's Word is that He does not give us that spirit, His gift to us is power, love and self-discipline, a sound mind, and sound/good judgement.

1 John 4:18 (ESV)

There is no fear in love, but perfect love casts out fear. For fear has to do with punishment, and whoever fears has not been perfected in love.

Did you notice the words 'cast out'? Yes those are active words which means you have to do something active to kick that joker out of your life. Fear is a spirit and through the authority of Jesus Christ it must be cast out. This means that walking in God's Spirit relying on the Holy Spirit will enable us to take control of those squatter thoughts and evict them.

The Merriam-Webster Dictionary **(1)** describes 'fear' as "an unpleasant often strong emotion caused by anticipation or awareness of danger, an instance of this emotion, a state marked by this emotion, anxious concern, a reason for alarm". The online medical dictionary **(2)** describes fear as "the emotional state consisting of psychological and physiological responses to a real external threat or danger, as the unpleasant emotional state consisting of psychological and psychophysiological responses to a real external threat or danger."

A spirit is a being without a body that targets you knowing your weak points and tries to stick to you through open doors. You have probably heard the acronym for fear: false evidence appearing real. This is exactly what it is; false evidence that incriminates you and makes you feel guilty and fearful all the time. Jesus showed us through His ministry that we are to cast out fear because it is a demonic spirit, not a feeling that makes us think there is something wrong with us. Oh and the other annoying thing is that loser fear likes to have his buddies join in on the party of harassing you. Often times where there is fear there are other demonic spirits that like to gang up and take you down (more of those other gang members coming up).

Granted the whole premise of this book and the sub title itself illustrates the fact that fear keeps us in bondage. It does not show up as a huge neon sign that points to the problem, its power is in its stealth and secrecy. We give power to fear by keeping the roots of fear secret and hidden. We break free from fear by confessing our sins, renouncing our iniquities, accepting mercy from God, and walking in faith.

Proverbs 28:13

Whoever conceals their sins does not prosper, but the one who confesses and renounces them finds mercy.

Unfortunately fear has written more prescriptions in modern society than we can count. Anxiety, depression, phobias, you name it; fear is the root of them all. It is thought to believe that there are 365 mentions of the term "fear not" in the bible **(3)**. That is one for every day of the year! God knew this is a troubling topic we grapple with and provides us the antidote in scripture for us to take our daily vitamin of fear nots.

Romans 10:17

So then faith comes by hearing, and hearing by the word of God.

The opposite of fear is faith. Fear has become habitual, so too does faith by us slowly creating new habits. This is how we dig ourselves out of the pit by regularly soaking our minds and hearts with the Word of God. One very important aspect to fighting fear is to realize that it can only operate through an open door. This means that either knowingly or unknowingly, you have allowed it access to your life through one or a variety of ways, and the only way to stop it is to slam those doors shut. We are going to delve deeper into these doors that you may have to work through to take back your authority and exercise your rights in Christ as a child of God.

Steps to break free from fear:

1) Begin with confession.

2) Name the fears by writing down the fear based thoughts to ditch the load.

3) Deal with the root cause and fix the fruit through repentance.

4) Worship is the playlist to fear.

Strategy:

The strategy we need is to take every thought captive as soon as it enters our minds. This sounds something like this; "You will always be too scared to do anything good… wait no that is not what God says about me. God does not give me a spirit of fear but of love, power and a sound mind. Fear be gone in Jesus name!" Stop the thought in its tracks. Allowing the negative tape to play over and over is just going to bully you into defeat. Press stop on those runaway thoughts before they take off and get flight.

Prayer: Release from Fear

Thank you Lord for your promise to deliver me when I call on your name. Please deliver me from the spirit of fear and break off any hold it has on me. I forgive every person that has hurt me and I release them in love. Release the dunamis power into every crevice of my broken soul and heal up the wounds of my past. I break and bind you spirit of fear be gone now in Jesus name amen!

Anxiety

Do not be anxious about anything, but in every situation, by prayer and petition, with thanksgiving, present your requests to God.

Philippians 4:6

Control Freaks Anonymous is recruiting for their team, are you already a member of the club? No do not answer that, it is probably why it is called the "anonymous" club. Confession time, I've been a member for many years and did not even know it. Now anxiety is no joking matter, it is a debilitating state of being that affects millions of people everyday. According to the Anxiety and Depression Association of America **(4)** "Anxiety disorders are the most common mental illness in the U.S., affecting 40 million adults in the United States age 18 and older, or 18.1% of the population every year. Anxiety disorders are highly treatable, yet only 36.9% of those suffering receive treatment."

Physical symptoms display themselves as stomach aches, lump in the throat, the fight or flight reaction, sweaty hands, irritability, attention deficit, the list goes on. Living in a constant state of fight or flight taxes our adrenal system and is not good for the body. A visit to a doctor made this abundantly clear when she said the stress from the anxiety I had been under was causing my body severe adverse effects. If I did not chill and learn to live at a normal rhythm, I could have long term ill effects. Anxiety is closely related to fear and worry (they all hang out together at the lunch table). The spirits of torment that are rooted in fear show themselves as anxiety and worry. They steal your peace and want to kill and destroy your joy.

The Office of the Surgeon General **(5)** conducted a study of combat soldiers who served in Iraq. The findings concluded that the level of combat was the main determinant of a soldiers mental health status. The length of deployment and family separations were considered the top mitigating factor, as does multiple deployments that showed higher acute stress and was related to higher rates of mental health problems and marital conflict. The suicide rates amongst combat soldiers was higher than the average army rate. PTSD is considered common place amongst those experiencing high levels of conflict, combat and threats to one's life.

In today's society our levels of stress are off the charts. Many individuals are displaying the same signs of stress that a soldier with PTSD who has been exposed to multiple stressors. The findings of a study **(6)** that appeared in the December issue of the American Psychological Association's (APA) Journal of Personality and Social Psychology said the average high school student today has the same level of anxiety as the average psychiatric patient had in the early 1950's! This is shocking.

The temporary emotion of anxiety is experienced as a reaction to a particular situation or perceived threat. With all the mod cons we have access to today we are suffering more than ever before. Excess causes anxiety. We are loaded with lists. Our clutter crushes our calm. We might be connected to thousands of "friends" on Facebook yet we are the most disconnected generation. We are creating less meaningful relationships and connections that the isolation is crushing our mental state of well being. The perceived threats we are exposed to due to information overload have contributed to this mental epidemic.

The Merriam-Webster dictionary defines the word anxious as "characterized by extreme uneasiness of mind or brooding fear about some contingency, ardently or earnestly wishing, characterized by, resulting from, or causing anxiety, worrying." Are you a brooder? Brooding is described as "moodily or sullenly thoughtful or serious, darkly somber." Wow are not we a bucket full of sunshine!

According to the World happiness report of 2017 **(7)** happiness is both social and personal. There are six variables that were measured to determine the index, and half were due to differences in having someone to count on, generosity, a sense of freedom, and freedom from corruption. In richer countries the differences were not explained only by income inequality, but by the differences in mental health, physical health and personal relationships. The study found that the largest single source of misery is mental illness. In 2007 the USA ranked 3rd among the OECD happiest countries where in 2016 it had dropped to 19th. In all three Western countries, diagnosed mental illness emerges as more important than income, employment or physical illness. You would think that eliminating poverty, unemployment and physical illness would be a huge factor, however these three factors barely make as much difference as mental illness on its own. The other eye opening finding is that in the USA, for example, a person who is poor is 5.5 percentage points more likely than otherwise to be miserable. By contrast someone with depression or anxiety is 10.7 percentage points more likely to be miserable.It costs money to reduce misery, but the cheapest of the policies is treating depression and anxiety disorders. Imagine if we could miraculously abolish depression and anxiety disorders without changing anything else?

An important factor they uncovered is that many of the problems of adulthood can be traced back to childhood and adolescence. The strongest predictor of a satisfying adult life is not qualifications but a combination of the child's emotional health and behaviour. The survey in the World Happiness report consisted of data compiled from a very detailed survey of all children born in the English County of Avon in 1991/2 who have been followed intensively up until today. The study compared family income, parenting style, parental engagement and involvement, and conflict between parents. They discovered that the worst factor of all for children's emotional health and behaviour is a mother who is mentally ill, more so than the fathers mental state. This means that us mothers have the most important influence on the future well being of our children, so we owe it to ourselves and our children to be healthy mentally.

Feeling anxious comes down to an issue of control. If we cannot control the outcome we get our knickers in a twist and freak out. If you notice the dictionary mentions "wishing". Anxiety is based on us worrying about some possible outcome that may or may not happen, wishing for the best. Last time I checked nobody got anything by "wishing".

God's Word is bursting with scriptures that says "don't be anxious" with 365 mentions in the bible; Philippians 4:6, Psalm 139:23, Ecclesiastes 2:22, Matthew 6:34, Luke 10:41, Luke 12:26, Matthew 6:31 to name a few.

If we do not deal with the root causes the tree of anxiety will keep on blooming. Let's be honest, the root cause of our anxiety is based in a deep seated distrust. What we are really saying when we are anxious is that we do not trust God to work things out for our good. We are not confident that He knows the best outcome for our lives and will do what He says He will do, so we prefer to brood about things and remain anxious. Perhaps it is a habit from your past and you do not know how else to live without feeling anxious about everything. The world (which is influenced by the devil) wants us to believe that anxiety is something we just have to live with. Many conditions are labeled as disorders when what they truly are is a demonic assault on our bodies, minds and souls to get us weak and wounded. We need to stop agreeing with the devil by accepting labels, conditions and disorders as normal; and start putting up a fight so we can get set free.

If we prefer to live our lives filled with fear and anxiety, then God cannot deliver us. We need to choose to let go and let God be the creator that we know Him to be, and let Him work things out. If you do not fully trust God then you need to dig deeper and ask why. As born again believers, if we believe that the bible is God's truth, then why do we take pieces but leave other pieces out? If God said "stop worrying I've got this" then we need to hand in our badge and retire our membership from the Control Freaks Anonymous club. Being set free from anxiety starts with developing an attitude of gratitude. We cannot be grateful and grumpy at the same time. Focusing on our blessings and the good things in life help us to reframe our thinking. What we focus on grows so feed your faith not your fears!

Prayer: Release from Anxiety

Thank you Lord for your unfailing love. I choose to place my trust in You. Please deliver me from anxiety and break off the spirit of fear. With your strength I take captive every negative thought that tries to steal my joy. I thank you Lord for delivering me from the spirit of fear and anxiety. In Jesus name amen!

Note: Always follow the advice of your medical practitioner when it comes to treating issues of anxiety and mental health.

Worry

Therefore I tell you, do not worry about your life, what you will eat or drink; or about your body, what you will wear, is not life more than food and the body more than clothes? Look at the birds of the air: They do not sow or reap or gather into barns—and yet your Heavenly Father feeds them. Are you not much more valuable than they?

Matthew 6: 25-26

Van Wilder said "Worrying is like a rocking chair, it gives you something to do, but doesn't get you anywhere." Joyce Meyer says "Worry is a down payment on a problem you may never have." I love this analogy because it is so true. When we worry we might think we are putting our energy to good use because there is lots of swaying back and forth, but at the end of the day we are still stuck in the exact same spot as when we started.

Worry is a gang member of that fear party, always trying to take us out using its fear tactics. For some of us it feels like worry has become part of our personality; "I'm a worry wart, I always worry about things, it is a family thing worrying all the time". Let me tell you sugar that is agreeing with the devil! Who in their right mind would want to willingly agree with the lie that worry is an effective use of energy? Saying words of worry and agreeing with the negative will only keep you stuck in that defeated cycle.

Matthew 6:27

Can all your worries add a single moment to your life?

The definition of 'worry' according to the The Merriam-Webster dictionary **(8)** is "to harass by tearing, biting, or snapping especially at the throat, to shake or pull at with the teeth a terrier worrying a rat, to touch or disturb something repeatedly, to change the position of or adjust by repeated pushing or hauling, to assail with rough or aggressive attack or treatment, to subject to persistent or nagging attention or effort, to afflict with mental distress or agitation, to make anxious, to torment."

Did you get that? Harassing, tearing, biting, snapping, shaking, pulling, disturbing, pushing, hauling, assail, rough, aggressive, attack, nagging, afflict, distress, agitation, torment. This sounds like a violent attack that can only result in the victim being destroyed, abused and even killed! Last time I checked the Bible there was zero, nil, zilch, nada times it mentions any of this as acceptable for God's children. In fact it says the exact opposite, so why would we willingly agree to this kind of treatment if we know that the only outcome is destruction? Get a grip girl!

Worry shows we that we do not trust God. Wow for God that is got to hurt! We know we are His child, yet we push away His hand of help because we do not trust Him enough to take care of our situation. Worrying about the future and things we cannot control robs us of today's blessings. Our bodies reflect our inner turmoil and worry exhibits itself in physical symptoms like headaches, stomach aches, loss of appetite, loss of sleep etc.

Proverbs 12:25

Worry weighs a person down; an encouraging word cheers a person up.

The truth of the matter is that no amount of worrying adds a single moment to our lives but takes away moments of joy, peace, faith and love. The opposite of worry is trust, peace, joy, patience, contentment, being even tempered and generally much more pleasant to get along with. Wouldn't you want that for your life? If you have decided enough is enough, you need to take an active role in casting out those punks of fear and worry.

Jesus said in Luke 12:4-7

4 "I tell you, my friends, do not be afraid of those who kill the body and after that can do no more. 5 But I will show you whom you should fear: Fear him who, after your body has been killed, has authority to throw you into hell. Yes, I tell you, fear him. 6 Are not five sparrows sold for two pennies? Yet not one of them is forgotten by God. 7 Indeed, the very hairs of your head are all numbered. Don't be afraid; you are worth more than many sparrows.

More references can be found in Luke 12:22-24, Matthew 6:25, Luke 21:14, and my favourite is;

2 Timothy 1:7

For God has not given us a spirit of fear, but of power and of love and of a sound mind.

As soon as you start feeling worried recognize it as a spirit out to torment you and use your mouth to speak God's truth from His Word. Speak 2 Timothy 1:7 scripture out loud to help you get the victory and start creating good thinking habits by taking every thought captive into the obedience of Christ.

Prayer: Release from Worry

Thank you Lord that your Word says that you don't give me a spirit of fear but divine power, love and a sound mind through Jesus. I thank you Lord that I can put my trust in You to work all things out for my good. I cast out the spirit of fear and worry and command it to go now in Jesus name. I plead the blood of Jesus over my mind and heart and protect myself with the armour of God so that I can fight off the attacks of the enemy. Thank you for delivering me in Jesus name amen!

Unforgiveness

If you forgive anyone, I also forgive him. And if I have forgiven anything, I have forgiven it in the presence of Christ for your sake.

2 Corinthians 2:10

Living with unforgiveness in our hearts is a root cause for many issues, illnesses, broken relationships and lost destinies. Holding grudges builds up a heaviness that follows us throughout life and opens the doors to a spirit of heaviness and many other tormenting spirits. Our bodies exhibit 'dis-ease' when our spirit and soul are not at peace. Many chronic diseases have been linked to unforgiveness. Jesus was very clear about the importance of forgiveness and how it impacts us personally.

Mark 11:25

And when you stand praying, if you hold anything against anyone, forgive them, so that your Father in heaven may forgive you your sins."

John 20:23

If you forgive anyone his sins, they are forgiven; if you withhold forgiveness from anyone, it is withheld.

Did you notice that part that said if you withhold forgiveness it is withheld from you? Wowza mind blown! Many prayers are left unanswered because God cannot permit an unforgiving heart to fester. He is a just and fair God and works through the protocol of heaven, which means we have to come before Him with pure hearts if we want our requests to be heard.

Have you ever felt like you have prayed and prayed about an issue, and yet you hear nothing? It seems like you are up against a brick wall, stainless steel door or glass ceiling? That is a classic sign that there is a spiritual block that needs to be removed and often it starts with unforgiveness. The sin of unforgiveness (and yes it is a sin) is insidious. It is one of those itty bitty seeds that starts so small, almost undetectable. At first "ping" it may not seem like a big deal, it starts with irritation and frustration, but left to fester it grows into a gigantic stronghold.

Matthew 18:15-17

15 "If your brother or sister sins, go and point out their fault, just between the two of you. If they listen to you, you have won them over. 16 But if they will not listen, take one or two others along, so that every matter may be established by the testimony of two or three witnesses. 17 If they still refuse to listen, tell it to the church; and if they refuse to listen even to the church, treat them as you would a pagan or a tax collector.

The parable of the unforgiving servant is a warning of the terrible consequences that can happen to us if we do not forgive another believer.

Matthew 18:23-35

23 Therefore the kingdom of heaven is like a certain king who wanted to settle accounts with his servants. 24 And when he had begun to settle accounts, one was brought to him who owed him ten thousand talents. 25 But as he was not able to pay, his master commanded that he be sold, with his wife and children and all that he had, and that payment be made. 26 The servant therefore fell down before him, saying, 'Master, have patience with me, and I will pay you all.' 27 Then the master of that servant was moved with compassion, released him, and forgave him the debt. 28 "But that servant went out and found one of his fellow servants who owed him a hundred denarii; and he laid hands on him and took him by the throat, saying, 'Pay me what you owe!' 29 So his fellow servant fell down at his feet and begged him, saying, 'Have patience with me, and I will pay you all. 30 And he would not, but went and threw him into prison till he should pay the debt. 31 So when his fellow servants saw what had been done, they were very grieved, and came and told their master all that had been done. 32 Then his master, after he had called him, said to him, 'You wicked servant! I forgave you all that debt because you begged me. 33 Should you not also have had compassion on your fellow servant, just as I had pity on you?' 34 And his master was angry, and delivered him to the torturers until he should pay all that was due to him. 35 "So My heavenly Father also will do to you if each of you, from his heart, does not forgive his brother his trespasses."

The failure to forgive others is also considered wickedness. The master in the parable said, "You wicked servant!" Unforgiveness is not merely a sin: it is wickedness. The Lord Jesus said God will treat you in the same way that the master in this story treated the unforgiving servant; He will deliver you to the tormentors (spiritual, mental, or physical). The lesson is clear that is if we do not forgive one another from the depths of our heart, then we will not be forgiven and will remain in torment. Being at the mercy of evil spirits means you lose your peace and joy, you will suffer from fear, and your mind will not be at rest. The only way you can get out of this torment jail is if you meet God's conditions for getting out. You cannot have true lasting peace, deliverance or freedom until you have freely forgiven everybody who has ever hurt you. This is God's unwavering condition, it is the only get out of jail card with no way around it.

Matthew 6:9 The Lord's prayer

If you do not forgive others, God does not forgive you. Do not deceive yourself—you are not forgiven by God. That is the source of all your problems. You do not have full forgiveness.

Christ has cleansed you from all unrighteousness and your forgiveness of sins is the reset button. Do not forget that the devil is a legalist and he knows if he has a legal claim over you if there is any area in your life where redemption's rights do not apply. You cannot get that punk out if there is any unforgiven sin in your life. No amount of shouting, jumping, binding, breaking, preaching or prayer will shake him loose if he has a legal right to be there. He is a persistent little pest who knows his rights, therefore the only way you can kick him out is with forgiveness. Think of forgiveness as an effective bug spray. You cannot obtain complete deliverance until you have applied the spray and freely forgiven anything and everything against anyone, person or thing.

It is not about whether you feel like it or not, you just have to decide. It is not a matter of emotions but your will. You do not have to feel forgiveness but you have to will forgiveness. As a born again child of God this will power already exists within you. Make up your mind today to forgive that person, institution or thing even if your emotions are screaming at you. It is simple; if you are to be forgiven then God requires that you forgive others. If you want your prayers to be answered you must forgive. If you want to experience freedom, joy, peace, and the fulfillment you were meant to have as a child of God, then forgiveness must become a habit. The choice is yours!

Ask the Holy Spirit to show you who you need to forgive (it may be something you have long forgotten about). The key is to be specific and name the person and the offense or hurt. It is a good idea to speak it out loud so your brain hears it. Once you have said it it is done, you do not have to repeat yourself and get all legalistic about it. However if you still feel resentment toward them, then start praying for the person as you cannot resent someone and pray for them at the same time. By praying you are replacing the negative with the positive.

Prayer: Release from Unforgiveness

Lord, I forgive _____ for _____ just as I want You to forgive me. Thank you for your forgiveness and redeeming me from my sins of unforgiveness. As an act of my will I release _____ (insert name) in forgiveness and pray your blessings over them/him/her. I declare the dunamis power is released into every area of my soul and body and is healing me right now. Please Lord release any blockages, holds, barriers and barricades that have hindered me from walking in your will for my life. Thank You in Jesus name amen!

Depression

I have cried until the tears no longer come; my heart is broken. My spirit is poured out in agony as I see the desperate plight of my people.

Lamentations 2:11

Depression is a condition that is not new. The bible references several famous bible characters that dealt with anxiety, despair and depression. David, Jonah, Job, Elijah, Moses, Jeremiah and even Jesus had to battle the giant of depression. David laments and the despair of Job can be identified as the "spirit of heaviness". It is like a heavy cloak that weighs us down.

David:

David wrote many of the Psalms David where he laments and cries out to God about his troubles, especially about the loss of his sons. You would think someone of his stature would not be vulnerable to depression but he struggled with it too.

2 Samuel 12:15-16

15 After Nathan had gone home, the Lord struck the child that Uriah's wife had borne to David, and he became ill. 16 David pleaded with God for the child. He fasted and spent the nights lying in sackcloth on the ground.

2 Samuel 18:33

The king was shaken. He went up to the room over the gateway and wept. As he went, he said: "O my son Absalom! My son, my son Absalom! If only I had died instead of you—O Absalom, my son, my son!

Psalm 143:7

Come quickly, LORD, and answer me, for my depression deepens. Don't turn away from me, or I will die.

Elijah:

The powerful prophet Elijah felt discouraged and wanted to die right afraid after winning a huge battle with Jezebel when he killed all the false prophets.

1 Kings 19:1-5

1 Now Ahab told Jezebel everything Elijah had done and how he had killed all the prophets with the sword. 2 So Jezebel sent a messenger to Elijah to say, "May the gods deal with me, be it ever so severely, if by this time tomorrow I do not make your life like that of one of them." 3 Elijah was afraid and ran for his life. When he came to Beersheba in Judah, he left his servant there, 4 while he himself went a day's journey into the wilderness. He came to a broom bush, sat down under it and prayed that he might die. "I have had enough, Lord," he said. "Take my life; I am no better than my ancestors." 5 Then he lay down under the bush and fell asleep.

Jonah:

The prophet Jonah was angry with God for His compassion toward the city of Nineveh and he wanted to rather die than do what God was telling him to.

Jonah 4:1-3

But to Jonah this seemed very wrong, and he became angry. 2 He prayed to the Lord, "Isn't this what I said, Lord, when I was still at home? That is what I tried to forestall by fleeing to Tarshish. I knew that you are a gracious and compassionate God, slow to anger and abounding in love, a God who relents from sending calamity. 3 Now, Lord, take away my life, for it is better for me to die than to live."

Jonah 4:9

But God said to Jonah, "Is it right for you to be angry about the plant?"
"It is," he said. "And I'm so angry I wish I were dead."

Job:

Job suffered utter devastation, massive losses and physical illness. This righteous man of God had lost literally everything from his children, his cattle and his home. His suffering and tragedy were so great that even his own wife said to him,

Job 2:9

"Are you still holding on to your integrity? Curse God and die!"

Job 30:16

And now my life seeps away. Depression haunts my days.

Moses:

The mighty man of God Moses was angry about the sin of his people and felt hopeless with how to help them.

Exodus 32:32

But now, please forgive their sin—but if not, then blot me out of the book you have written."

Jeremiah:

Jeremiah wrestled with insecurity, loneliness, and feeling defeated. He regretted the day he was born.

Jeremiah 20:14,18

"Cursed be the day I was born...why did I ever come out of the womb to see trouble and sorrow and to end my days in shame?"

Jesus:

Jesus Himself was deeply anguished and grieved over the suffering He knew He had to go through that He sweated blood.

Isaiah 53:3

He was despised and rejected by mankind, a man of suffering, and familiar with pain. Like one from whom people hide their faces he was despised, and we held him in low esteem.

Mark 14:34-36

34 And He said to them, "My soul is deeply grieved to the point of death; remain here and keep watch." 35 And He went a little beyond them, and fell to the ground and began to pray that if it were possible, the hour might pass Him by. 36 And He was saying, "Abba! Father! All things are possible for You; remove this cup from Me; yet not what I will, but what You will."

Luke 22:44

And being in anguish, he prayed more earnestly, and his sweat was like drops of blood falling to the ground.

Depression is a very common, yet a very treatable condition that affects many people in the world. According to WebMd **(9)** the causes of depression are abuse, medications, relational conflict, death or loss, genetics, major life events, personal problems, serious illness, and substance abuse.

If you or a loved one is struggling with suicidal thoughts and tendencies please get help. Call the National Suicide Prevention Hotline at

1-800-273-TALK (8255) (USA) at any time day or night 24/7, or go online at www.suicidepreventionlifeline.org for more information and help.

The definition of depression from the Merriam-Webster dictionary **(10)** is; "an act of depressing or a state of being depressed: such as a state of feeling sad, dejection anger, anxiety, and depression. A mood disorder marked especially by sadness, inactivity, difficulty in thinking and concentration, a significant increase or decrease in appetite and time spent sleeping, feelings of dejection and hopelessness, and sometimes suicidal tendencies bouts of depression suffering from clinical depression. A reduction in activity, amount, quality, or force a depression in trade. A lowering of physical or mental vitality or of functional activity, a pressing down."

What does the bible say about depression? Depression is a manifestation of a tormenting spirit that is often a result from family genetics, or from an open door caused by trauma. We can be delivered from this tormenting, heavy, oppressive spirit that holds us down and keeps us captive because through Jesus we have authority over all tormenting spirits to cast them out. Do not accept it as just a feeling, use your authority in Jesus Christ to overcome the tormentor by asking for forgiveness for your sins and allowing the Holy Spirit to heal your heart.

1 Samuel 16:14

Now the Spirit of the LORD had left Saul, and the LORD sent a tormenting spirit that filled him with depression and fear.

1 Samuel 16:23 (NLT)

And whenever the tormenting spirit from God troubled Saul, David would play the harp. Then Saul would feel better, and the tormenting spirit would go away.

God's promise is clear that He will give us beauty in exchange for our ashes. It starts with changing the way you think. Every negative suggestion or thought that pops in your head must immediately be counteracted with a positive thought. It can takes years to undo negative thinking especially if it has become habitual, but we can reprogram the mind with proper training and daily soaking in God's Word. It doesn't matter what the devil does or the world says, God has the last word and His Word is the medicine for our afflictions. It goes to show that we are all flawed, yet no matter who we are, God can still use us and turn our situation around.

Isaiah 61:3 (NLT)

To all who mourn in Israel, he will give a crown of beauty for ashes, a joyous blessing instead of mourning, festive praise instead of despair. In their righteousness, they will be like great oaks that the LORD has planted for his own glory.

We are equipped to fight this fight by being doers of the Word and not just passive listeners. We are to wear the helmet of hope which is the helmet of salvation. When we know that we are saved we do not have to rely on our works, our efforts or some magical incantation to be set free. The moment we are saved we are given the keys to unlock our prison doors from the inside. We permanently have an insider who knows how to navigate out the prison maze and help us escape to find the light. That insider is the Holy Spirit.

Allowing thoughts of worthlessness will overwhelm our minds. Our rejection and frustration then turns into disappointment. Our disappointment then turns to despair, then to depression, and then to thoughts of suicide and even death. A lack of hope, a lack of vision, and a lack of purpose are at the crux of the matter.

Proverbs 13:12

Hope deferred makes the heart sick, but a longing fulfilled is a tree of life.

The remedy for this oppression is that our world desperately need more joy, hope and grace and the reminder that our lasting help is found only in Jesus. We counteract depression with joy because the joy of the Lord is our strength! Even if you don't 'feel' joyful you decide you want to be joyful and meditate on God's Word until the joy fills you with strength. Often this means turning up the volume on praise and worship music and shaking it off on the dance floor.

Psalm 30:11

You have turned my mourning into joyful dancing. You have taken away my clothes of mourning and clothed me with joy.

By studying the Word we learn how to distinguish between a thought that comes from our own mind, and those injected by a demonic spirit. Every time the enemy tries to weigh us down with negative or pessimistic thinking, we need to discipline ourselves to counteract this attack with a positive word from scripture. God's Word spoken out loud is our remedy. Wielding the sword of the spirit is our weapon of mass destruction!

If we can keep our eyes fixed on Jesus, the author and finisher of our faith, instead of our circumstances; we can take back our authority. God does not want you languishing in depression, tormented by this heavy spirit, and disabled from achieving your destiny. The solution is clear and very simple, call on the name of the Lord to rescue you. Ask for forgiveness of all sins and renounce your negative thoughts and words when you have agreed with the enemy. Accept you are saved and delivered and be set free!

Prayer: Release from Depression

Thank You Jesus for dying for me and for Your victory on the cross. I declare that I have been released from the torment, and that my spirit, body, and soul are willing vessels of righteousness, completely surrendered to God for His service and His glory. In Jesus name amen!

Self Pity

You said, 'Woe to me! The LORD has added sorrow to my pain; I am worn out with groaning and find no rest.'

Jeremiah 45:3

In the story of Elijah we see that after he fought a tough battle he went alone into the wilderness. After traveling all day he sat down under a tree and prayed that he might die.

1 Kings 19:1-9,

1 Now Ahab told Jezebel everything Elijah had done and how he had killed all the prophets with the sword. 2 So Jezebel sent a messenger to Elijah to say, "May the gods deal with me, be it ever so severely, if by this time tomorrow I do not make your life like that of one of them." 3 Elijah was afraid and ran for his life. When he came to Beersheba in Judah, he left his servant there, 4 while he himself went a day's journey into the wilderness. He came to a broom bush, sat down under it and prayed that he might die. "I have had enough, Lord," he said. "Take my life; I am no better than my ancestors." 5 Then he lay down under the bush and fell asleep.

All at once an angel touched him and said, "Get up and eat." 6 He looked around, and there by his head was some bread baked over hot coals, and a jar of water. He ate and drank and then lay down again. 7 The angel of the Lord came back a second time and touched him and said, "Get up and eat, for the journey is too much for you." 8 So he got up and ate and drank. Strengthened by that food, he traveled forty days and forty nights until he reached Horeb, the mountain of God. 9 There he went into a cave and spent the night.

Elijah wasn't the only one who had a pity party, we see it in Job too.

Job 19:21

Have pity on me, my friends, have pity, for the hand of God has struck me.

David also found himself in a pity party;

Psalm 10:1

O LORD, why do you stand so far away? Why do you hide when I am in trouble?

And we cannot forget the most notable instance of Jesus who felt forsaken by God,

Matthew 27:46

About three in the afternoon Jesus cried out in a loud voice, "Eli, Eli, lema sabachthani?" (which means "My God, my God, why have you forsaken me?").

As we can see with all these accounts is the fact that each of them found themselves feeling forsaken and alone. When we are isolated from others we have too much time to focus on our own situation and all the woes that come with it. A pity party is a party of one and you're the only one invited! No one wants to be company for someone who is negative, complaining and wallowing in self pity. Granted, all of us have times when we experience terrible circumstances that make us feel alone, and all that we know to do is to resort to self pity. Having a pity party is like a toddler pouting and sulking when they do not get their way because their focus is "me me me". We need to decide to stop using self pity as a badge of honor to get attention as no one gets any benefit from it, mostly notably you.

The first tip we can learn from these scriptures is to not isolate ourselves. Having a friend to talk with and share your load goes a long way to alleviating your feelings of abandonment. However it is important not to delve into the drama and talk about it over and over again, that will just keep you stuck. We are the air traffic controller of our lives, we decide what planes are allowed to land and deliver their cargo. Do not let bad cargo the chance to unpack and dump its dirty drama all over your day.

Life comes with lemons but we have a choice whether or not to let them sour our lives. Our decision tree of daily choices is determined by our ability to see the wood for the trees. It is our decision to sit under the shade of a tree of tranquility or anxiety. God's Word gives us everything we need and shows us that we do not have to feel alone and rely on ourselves.

Psalm 23 :1-6

1 The Lord is my shepherd, I lack nothing. 2 He makes me lie down in green pastures, he leads me beside quiet waters, he refreshes my soul. He guides me along the right paths for his name's sake. 4 Even though I walk through the darkest valley, I will fear no evil, for you are with me; your rod and your staff, they comfort me. 5 You prepare a table before me in the presence of my enemies. You anoint my head with oil; my cup overflows. 6 Surely your goodness and love will follow me all the days of my life, and I will dwell in the house of the Lord forever.

Prayer: Release from Self Pity

Thank you God that your Word says you are my shepherd who guides me so I never need to feel alone. Thank you that I lack nothing and for your comfort during dark days. Thank you for making me calm and refreshing my soul. Thank you for protecting me from the enemy. Please Lord forgive me of my sins of selfishness. As an act of my will I choose to focus on you and not my circumstances and I reject all forms of self pity. Thank you for delivering me in Jesus name amen!

Guilt, Shame and Condemnation

So now there is no condemnation for those who belong to Christ Jesus.

Romans 8:1

In the garden of Eden after Eve took the bait from Satan and ate the apple, the first thing they experienced was a sense of shame. Before their sin Adam and Eve were not aware that they were naked, and had no shame. As soon as they sinned shame came barreling in. When God came to walk with them in the garden they hid in the bushes. God knew exactly what they had done but in His grace He was giving them a chance to fess up. Let us look at the story here;

Genesis 3: 1-13

1 Now the serpent was more crafty than any of the wild animals the Lord God had made. He said to the woman, "Did God really say, 'You must not eat from any tree in the garden'?" 2 The woman said to the serpent, "We may eat fruit from the trees in the garden, 3 but God did say, 'You must not eat fruit from the tree that is in the middle of the garden, and you must not touch it, or you will die.'" 4 "You will not certainly die," the serpent said to the woman. 5 "For God knows that when you eat from it your eyes will be opened, and you will be like God, knowing good and evil." 6 When the woman saw that the fruit of the tree was good for food and pleasing to the eye, and also desirable for gaining wisdom, she took some and ate it. She also gave some to her husband, who was with her, and he ate it. 7 Then the eyes of both of them were opened, and they realized they were naked; so they sewed fig leaves together and made coverings for themselves. 8 Then the man and his wife heard the sound of the Lord God as he was walking in the garden in the cool of the day, and they hid from the Lord God among the trees of the garden. 9 But the Lord God called to the man, "Where are you?" 10 He answered, "I heard you in the garden, and I was afraid because I was naked; so I hid." 11 And he said, "Who told you that you were naked? Have you eaten from the tree that I commanded you not to eat from?" 12 The man said, "The woman you put here with me—she gave me some fruit from the tree, and I ate it." 13 Then the Lord God said to the woman, "What is this you have done?" The woman said, "The serpent deceived me, and I ate."

Did you notice the first thing Satan did was to get Eve to question God? Then he got her to think that God was holding out on her by not letting her have access to the knowledge of the tree. One bite and whoosh, their eyes are opened. They were ashamed by their nakedness and they hid. Once the gig was up and they got caught in their sin, they turned on each other and started blaming one another.

What we can learn is that the power of sin is in its secrecy. When we sin, or someone sins against us, it immediately breeds a spirit of shame to keep the sin hidden. When things are hidden they are not exposed to the light, and cannot receive the healing it need. Our secrets make us sick physically, mentally, emotionally and spiritually. Unresolved guilt and shame causes anxiety when we work to try and keep sins hidden. When we deny the truth and allow shame and condemnation to set in, we find ourselves stuck. Condemnation is a big buddy of shame, they like to harass us into silence.

If you have experienced any abuse, molestation, rape or any kind of hurt; firstly I am so sorry for your pain. When someone sins against us in such cases it is unfair especially when the sin was committed against our will. The good news is that you do not have to continue living in guilt and shame because Jesus paid the price to set you free.

Romans 5:18

Yes, Adam's one sin brings condemnation for everyone, but Christ's one act of righteousness brings a right relationship with God and new life for everyone.

There is a difference between condemnation and conviction. With conviction the Holy Spirit is gently reminding us that what we said or did, or omitted to say or do, is not in line with God's will. This gentle conviction is to usher us into forgiveness so we can release ourselves from any accusations the enemy wants to hold against us. While condemnation is a direct assault from the devil to keep us bound, wounded and offended so we never break free from his slimy grip. Condemnations voice usually sounds like this "You are a terrible person", where conviction will sound like this "What you did was terrible". The focus of conviction is to highlight the errors of our ways so we can get into right standing with God. This is so simple as all we have to do is say "God I am sorry forgive me". If you find yourself bombarded with condemning thoughts that make you feel bad about yourself and make you feel trapped, you need to kick that harassing spirit out of your mind!

Romans 8:1

Therefore, there is now no condemnation for those who are in Christ Jesus.

Prayer: Release from guilt, shame, condemnation

Dear Lord, thank You that your Word says there is no condemnation for those who are in Christ Jesus. As a child of God I claim my inheritance of love, joy and peace for I have the mind of Christ. I forgive those who have sinned and hurt me. I command the spirit of fear, guilt, shame and condemnation to flee now in Jesus name. Thank you for the gift of freedom in Jesus. I receive your grace Lord and healing in my body and soul. In Jesus name amen!

Jealousy

Therefore as surely as I live, declares the Sovereign LORD, I will treat you in accordance with the anger and jealousy you showed in your hatred of them and I will make myself known among them when I judge you.

Ezekiel 35:11

Feeling a little jelly lately? Has the green eyed monster grabbed your attention? When you are surfing on social media do you feel a little jealous when you see your friends basking in the sun on some tropical vacation, or have perfectly quaffed outfits in family photos, or look like their lives are so perfectly together? The problem is that being jealous does not make you feel good about yourself, you end up in the comparison trap. Comparison is the thief of joy so if you are feeling sad or depressed, maybe you have been spending too much time comparing yourself to those show reels on Facebook. The reality is that no one has a perfect life, you never know what they are going through behind-the-scenes because most of us filter our lives and keep everyone on a need to know basis. We need to keep that perspective and remind ourselves to be grateful so we can avoid the jelly zone.

The definition of jealousy is **(11)** a hostility toward a rival or one believed to enjoy an advantage, envious, intolerant of rivalry, unfaithfulness, disposed to suspect rivalry, vigilant in guarding a possession. Crimes of passion have been committed due to jealousy. Like anger, a jealous rage blinds the reasoning and flips the switch on clear thinking.

James 3:16

For where you have envy and selfish ambition, there you find disorder and every evil practice.

It's important to build the habit of being grateful instead of jealous. When you see someone who appears to enjoy life a little sweeter than you, pray for them and thank God that you have the blessings you have. You cannot be grateful and jealous at the same time, so put your focus back where it belongs on praising Jesus for the sacrifice He made for you.

Prayer: Release from Jealousy

Dear Lord I thank you for the sacrifice Jesus made for me to be free. I repent of the sin of jealousy. I am grateful for all my blessings and put my trust in you God to pour the blessings into my life that you have planned for me. I repent of the negative words I've spoken over others in my jealous state, and cancel their ill effects in Jesus name amen!

6. Barriers in The Mouth

Negative Words

Wise words bring approval, but fools are destroyed by their own words.

Ecclesiastes 10:12

God created the world with His words, Jesus cursed the fig tree with His words and it withered. Our words are containers of power!

Proverbs 18:21

Death and life are in the power of the tongue: and they that love it shall eat the fruit thereof.

Our mouth gets us in a whole lot of trouble. We can determine the success of our day by how we speak. We can live the results of our withered or fruitful words. We can immediately tell the health of a person's soul by the standard of their speech. A wounded soul speaks out of the mouth;

Matthew 15:18

But the things that come out of a person's mouth come from the heart, and these defile them.

It is critical that we censor our speech. Just like Jesus caused the tree to wither, our withering words can cause the fruits of our gifts, talents, relationships, and future to wither. Lies and omission of truths also fall within the category of negative words, sometimes it is not what we say but also what we do not say that keeps us stuck. We have the power to loose or bind on earth what it is in heaven. We cannot take back words once the damage is done, but we can use our words by agreeing with God's Word to bring health and healing.

As a modern society we use colloquial words as part of our everyday speech and we have become blinded by their power. For example, do you find yourself saying things like ; "I'm dying to", "you're killing me", "I'm sick and tired", "you're dead to me", "you're driving me crazy", "I'm losing my sanity" etc.? We have become so flippant with our speech that we have become numb to their negative effects. They are not humorous sayings as the devil is not laughing but takes us seriously by our choice of words. We may think they make us look or sound cool, but it is not cool when the devil messes with us because we have allowed him free reign through our flippant speech.

Perhaps you have pronouncing word curses over yourself and did not even know it. Have you been part of a group, society, fraternity, or sorority where you have had to make vows as part of your initiation or acceptance? Have you considered the power of the words that you have so easily agreed to? The enemy loves to disguise his tactics in "white lies" and non threatening agreements that seem, at first glance, harmless. But by no means are they harmless when they have given legal ground for the devil to infiltrate your life! A marriage vow is considered a sacred event when two souls agree with their mouths to be married and tied together for life. God takes vows very seriously.

Deuteronomy 23:21

If you make a vow to the LORD your God, do not be slow to pay it, for the LORD your God will certainly demand it of you and you will be guilty of sin.

We can use our words to judge and condemn people without knowing it. Teasing and using sarcastic words in jest also has a significant impact on the recipient and the speaker. No one likes to be on the receiving end of being teased or belittled, and sarcasm is just a cowards way to hide their own insecurities. God's Word is clear: we are to love and not judge. Only God is permitted to judge the hearts of man of those that reject Jesus.

John 12: 47-49

47 If anyone hears my words but does not keep them, I do not judge that person. For I did not come to judge the world, but to save the world. 48 There is a judge for the one who rejects me and does not accept my words; the very words I have spoken will condemn them at the last day. 49 For I did not speak on my own, but the Father who sent me commanded me to say all that I have spoken.

We have talked about the need to tame the tongue now let us look at how you can wield the power of your words. Agree with God's Word not mans. You do not have to agree with the death nature of negative words or a bad diagnosis. Stop agreeing with the negative words and start speaking God's Word into a situation.

Proverbs 4:23

Above all else, guard your heart, for everything you do flows from it.

Prayer: Release from Negative Words

Dear Lord please forgive the negative and destructive words I have spoken against myself and others. I cancel all curses and negative consequences that have results from my negative speech. Please forgive me for agreeing with the enemy and speaking words of death and destruction. I declare that I made in the image of God, I have the mind of Christ, by Jesus stripes I am healed, and I live in my inheritance of love, joy and peace in the Holy Spirit. In Jesus name amen!

Judgement and Criticism

Don't condemn others, and God won't condemn you. God will be as hard on you as you are on others!

Matthew 7 :1-5

God's Word is clear do not judge lest you be judged. Why do we focus on the speck in our sisters eye when we have a log in our own? Judging others is based on our own small view of the world. We judge and criticize what we do not understand, thinking that we are better than everyone else because of our own beliefs, experiences and convictions. The difference between judging by the spirit of God is judging between what is right or wrong based on God's Word. Judging and criticizing out of our own opinions shows that we have a spirit of pride and self righteousness that is not based on God's Word.

Luke 6:37

Do not judge, and you will not be judged. Do not condemn, and you will not be condemned. Forgive, and you will be forgiven.

In God's economy there is a principle of checks and balances that is determined by our choices. If we choose to judge and criticize others, we will be left to deal with the consequences of judgement upon ourselves. If we choose to show mercy and kindness to others, even when they do not deserve it, we are opening the doors to God's blessings and favour. Granted, God says we are to test every spirit so that we may know what is of God and what is not, so we can avoid being duped by false teachings.

1 John 4:1-2

1 Dear friends, do not believe every spirit, but test the spirits to see whether they are from God, because many false prophets have gone out into the world. 2 This is how you can recognize the Spirit of God: Every spirit that acknowledges that Jesus Christ has come in the flesh is from God.

Did you notice though that this kind of judgement has nothing to do with judging sinners? Jesus came to save the sinners not to judge them, so why do we feel justified to cast our judgement and criticize those that need Jesus the most? God's Word is abundantly clear that we are to get rid of judgements and have clean hands and a pure heart.

Psalm 24:4

The one who has clean hands and a pure heart, who does not trust in an idol or swear by a false god.

As a child I remember our church Sunday School handing out bracelets with the acronym WWJD (What Would Jesus Do). It was used in teaching kids how to act like Jesus. I remember wearing the bracelet and it proved to be a very useful tool in reminding me to think first about how Jesus would act, before opening my big mouth. As adults we could use this reminder too before we open our mouths and spew judgment and criticism. Walking in love not judgement will set us free from the bondages we create for ourselves by our loose speech.

Matthew 7 :1-5

Don't condemn others, and God won't condemn you. God will be as hard on you as you are on others! He will treat you exactly as you treat them. You can see the speck in your friend's eye, but you don't notice the log in your own eye. How can you say, "My friend, let me take the speck out of your eye," when you don't see the log in your own eye? You're nothing but show-offs! First, take the log out of your own eye. Then you can see how to take the speck out of your friend's eye.

James 4:11

Don't speak evil against each other, dear brothers and sisters. If you criticize and judge each other, then you are criticizing and judging God's law. But your job is to obey the law, not to judge whether it applies to you.

God is clear that as children of God He expects more of us. Behaving like petty school yard kids pecking at each other is disobedience. Talking behind the back of someone is bringing judgment upon yourself. Did you notice the part about "God will be as hard on you as you are on others"? Ouch that is scary stuff! The dangerous thing about judging and condemning others is we are writing our own sentence for bondage. If you have wondered why your prayers are not being answered, why you do not seem to get a breakthrough no matter how hard you pray; then perhaps you should consider if your mouth has got you into trouble. Quickly come before the Lord and repent so that you can be released from your prison of condemnation.

Prayer: Release from Judgement & Condemnation

Dear Lord thank You for Your mercy and kindness. I ask for forgiveness for the words I've said and thoughts I've had in judgment and criticism towards _____ (insert name/s). Please forgive me I repent of my sins, please release me from bondage. In Jesus name amen!

Offense

Point out anything in me that offends you, and lead me along the path of everlasting life.

Psalm 139:24

One of the biggest tools that Satan loves to use against us in the courts of Heaven is to accuse us of being offended by someone else. Now for many of us we, myself included, have been guilty of this. Getting offended, having our feelings hurt, and then harboring a grudge towards someone (whether it be my own family, someone I love, or a Christian) keeps us stuck.

Of course this is Satan's ultimate plan, to keep us out of the will of God, keeping us unprotected and making us vulnerable so he can attack us. And let me tell you darlings, if you have allowed any offense to get deep within your soul and you still hold grudges and hurt feelings, when you talk about it or think about it you will feel the same emotions you did the day you were hurt. This is a true sign that you have not truly forgiven. We can forgive with our minds, but unless it is an choice of our hearts the only true litmus test is to see if you can think and talk about the situation without feeling hurt. How does it make you feel? Our bodies are connected to our soul and our spirit. Even though you might think that you have forgiven the person, if you still have any feelings of animosity towards them it will keep you stuck in the mud. Offense is one primary sin that wounds people making them physically sick. Offense is like a reverse arrow that penetrates the heart and leaves gaping wounds in the heart of the offended.

The issue with offense is that if you have an offense against someone you are opening up a case file in the Courts of Heaven. We are filling the courts of Heaven with arguments that are keeping cases open in small claims court wasting Heavens time and resources. So let's stop it now. We can rectify the situation and settle the matter out of court without causing any strain on Heavenly resources. We are delaying our own blessings so it is important that we walk through forgiving those who have offended us.

God's Word is clear and says to go to your brother and ask for forgiveness and repair the relationship. Joyce Meyer likes to say, "Before going to the phone, you need to go to the throne." Before you gossip and complain to a friend about someone, how so-and-so hurt your feelings; you need to go to Heaven and ask God first. This is an act of humility. A simple prayer like "God please forgive me. Show me where I have been wrong" is very effective. You can only control your own behaviour and your own thoughts, you cannot control someone else's behaviour and thoughts about you. This is where we need to learn to let it go and say, "Lord, you be my advocate even though I feel unjustifiably accused of this" and God will be your vindicator. The is when it takes a step of faith knowing that God is our protector and Jesus is our advocate, He will stand up for us. Allowing Him to step instead of our situation is far easier than making more of a mess trying to handle things ourselves. Now that we have uncovered how offense can keep us stuck, let us pray together to be release from it.

Prayer: Release from Offense

Dear Lord Jesus, please forgive me for any offense I've had against any person, living or dead. Please allow me to release them in love. Heal my heart from any hurts. Seal up any holes that have opened up and close any ways that Satan has access to. Fill me with your love Lord Jesus, from the tip of my head to the soles of my toes. Your perfect love will cast out all fear. I accept the fact that I have been hurt, but I will not allow that to stick to my spirit and my heart. I release them now in Jesus name. Lord, loose me from any feelings of animosity or any resentment. It will it to be gone out of my life. In Jesus name amen!

Now that you have prayed, you need to stop talking about it and stop thinking about it. Turn the page and start a new chapter in your life. Make the conscious choice that if somebody does not agree with you, or someone hurts your feelings, that very instant you will forgive them. You are not to stew on it and think about it, or replay the conversation over and over in your mind, or talk about it with someone else, okay?

Congrats you have given yourself a spiritual shower! It is better to deal with each instant of hurt or offense immediately instead of allowing things to build up and fester. As you know when you leave something to rot, that one bad apple can affect the whole batch. So do not allow the bad apples to even begin rotting. Throw them out before they get a chance to fester. This is why it is so important that we renew our mind on a daily basis, we ask for forgiveness on a daily basis. It is not just a once and done approach. It is a continual lifestyle just like when we are encouraged by a health provider to get daily exercise. Thanking God for what He has done and asking for His forgiveness for any sin committed knowingly and unknowingly, will release you immediately.

Often times we can say things to people and not even realize that we have hurt them, so the cycle of offense continues with their offense against us. We might be thinking it is all hunky dory, but if we have offended somebody in any shape or form, they are holding offense against us. So once again we are dragged into the courts of heaven. If that person keeps hold of the offense it is another barrier to blessing. This does not mean that if they refuse to forgive you that you will never be forgiven, each of us is responsible for our own faith walk. It just creates unnecessary "paperwork" for both parties. This is a big reason why we need to be mindful of our words (more on this topic coming up in a later section). Asking for forgiveness means putting our pride in our pocket and humbling ourselves. We heal and repair bridges this way and is often the easiest solution to any conflict. So I have learnt to pray like this on a daily basis,

Daily Prayer for Offense:

God, please forgive me for any sin with what I have said, knowingly or unknowingly, and reveal to me where I have erred so that I can repair what is broken and ask for forgiveness.

How many movies have you watched and know of family situations where people go on for years not speaking to each other? Somebody said something back in the day and years later they cannot remember what the argument was about. How ridiculous! How many years has the locust stolen? How many loving relationships have been spoiled because they have allowed pride and resentment to stew? It is sad to see this even amongst Christians, where if anyone comes against us and our beliefs we get easily offended. Do not get me started with politics either!

How do you behave behind closed doors? Do you talk negatively about people who have offended you? Do you say "bless her heart" to her face then go straight behind her back and gossip and judge and criticize? Ouch! Ladies that is not the kind of behaviour that is fitting for a lady who is God's ambassador.

Remember too that being right is overrated. For someone who is very headstrong I like to be opinionated, and I admit I do not like being told when I am wrong. But I have matured a lot over the years and often I find it easier just to say, "I have my point of view, the other person has their point of view. Let us just agree to disagree". This can be the easiest way to release you from a whole lot of trouble.

Offense is the bait of Satan according to author John Bevere **(1)**. Do not take the bait and allow offense to hijack your heart and your emotions. Complaining about the speck in your sisters eye when you have a huge log in yours in hypocritical. Instead of sticking our fingers in the other person's eye we should rather grab their hand and walk with them.

Taking offense leads to defense and barricades us in prison of our own understanding. Just do like Elsa and let it go!

Prayer: Release from Offense

Lord, I forgive _____ for offending me and ask that you forgive me for holding grudges and offense. Thank you for your forgiveness of my sins and redeeming me through Jesus blood sacrifice. In Jesus name amen!

Complaining

Do everything without grumbling or arguing.

Philippians 2 :14

Complaining, grumbling and negative talk is another way our mouth gets us into trouble. When we complain, we shut down the heavens over us. I like to imagine it is like I'm praying for an answer to prayer, and God has sent my answer in the form of a package ready to be delivered to my address. Every time I complain it hits the pause button on the conveyor belt of progress, and my package gets delayed. Often my package gets delivered but I am so busy fretting on Worry Way, grumbling on Lament Lane or complaining on Complaints Corner that I am not home to receive it. Sometimes if my complaints are so bad, my behaviour might end up sending the package back to sender! All jokes aside, complaining and grumbling shows that we are ungrateful and being ungrateful is a sign of spiritual immaturity. Every time I take my eyes off Jesus and forget to be grateful, I delay its delivery and have to start all over again. God is clear about his view on our grumbling and complaining, we are to come to Jesus and value discipline and correction so we will find honor.

John 6:43-44

"Stop grumbling among yourselves," Jesus answered. "No one can come to me unless the Father who sent me draws them, and I will raise them up at the last day."

Prayer: Release from Complaining

Dear Lord I thank you for Jesus and that I can keep my eyes fixed on Him. I repent of my complaining and grumbling, I am grateful for all my blessings. I cancel all negative effects my complaints have caused, and I open the heavens over my situation. Thank you Lord you are loosing and releasing the answer to my prayers in Jesus name amen!

Religious Spirit

But when the teachers of religious law who were Pharisees saw him eating with tax collectors and other sinners, they asked his disciples, "Why does he eat with such scum?"

Mark 2:16

Saul who became Paul was a legalistic man bent on killing anyone who did not agree with his beliefs and values. Christians were at the top of his hit list and Saul was responsible for the murder of many believers. However, one touch from God and he became a changed man.

Acts 9: 1-6

1 Meanwhile, Saul was still breathing out murderous threats against the Lord's disciples. He went to the high priest 2 and asked him for letters to the synagogues in Damascus, so that if he found any there who belonged to the Way, whether men or women, he might take them as prisoners to Jerusalem. 3 As he neared Damascus on his journey, suddenly a light from heaven flashed around him. 4 He fell to the ground and heard a voice say to him, "Saul, Saul, why do you persecute me?" 5 "Who are you, Lord?" Saul asked. "I am Jesus, whom you are persecuting," he replied. 6 "Now get up and go into the city, and you will be told what you must do."

During Jesus's era the Pharisees were considered the most religious and highly respected men of their time, but they were responsible for Jesus's arrest and crucifixion. Legalism keeps people in bondage. Religiosity keeps us blinded to the truth. Jesus showed us that self righteous people are the hardest to reach because they do not think they need saving. Sinners know they need saving and humble themselves by asking for forgiveness and receive the gifts freely. God's strength is made perfect in our weakness. This means that only when we truly rely on Him, can we do all things through Christ so that God gets the glory.

Luke 18: 10-14

10 "Two men went up to the temple to pray, one a Pharisee and the other a tax collector. 11 The Pharisee stood by himself and prayed: 'God, I thank you that I am not like other people—robbers, evildoers, adulterers—or even like this tax collector. 12 I fast twice a week and give a tenth of all I get.' 13 "But the tax collector stood at a distance. He would not even look up to heaven, but beat his breast and said, 'God, have mercy on me, a sinner.' 14 "I tell you that this man, rather than the other, went home justified before God. For all those who exalt themselves will be humbled, and those who humble themselves will be exalted."

Jesus called the Pharisees a brood of vipers because they were all talk and no action, piously spewing their judgement and criticism toward others. They were more concerned about appearances and good works, and their pride was distasteful to Jesus.

Matthew 23:13

13 "Woe to you, teachers of the law and Pharisees, you hypocrites! You shut the door of the kingdom of heaven in people's faces. You yourselves do not enter, nor will you let those enter who are trying to.

Here we have the issue of the mouth once again. If we cannot tame our tongue and refrain from judging others according to our impossible standards of religion, we end up deceived.

James 1:26

Those who consider themselves religious and yet do not keep a tight rein on their tongues deceive themselves, and their religion is worthless.

Our blind spots blind us to having a religious spirit because we base our faith on works and not grace. This keeps us in bondage because we can never do enough and be enough without Jesus. That is why we need a saviour! Jesus died so we can have a real relationship with Him, not so we have to live according to a list of religious to do's. Going to church (check), wearing my Sunday best (check), saying my prayers every night (check). God is not interested in whether you can behave well enough to be worthy to enter His presence, He gave us the free ticket through Jesus. It's a gift and all you need to do is receive it.

Prayer: Release from Religious Spirit

Dear Lord thank you for the redeeming power of the cross. I repent of judging and criticizing others according to a set of man made rules. I break off the spirit of religion off myself and my generational line. I cancel all curses of disobedience and pride due to the spirit of religion. Thank you God that you are lifting the veil off my eyes and my loved ones so that your message grace is revealed to our hearts in Jesus name amen!

7. Unleashing the Warrior

Unleashing the Warrior

For we wrestle not against flesh and blood, but against principalities, against powers, against the rulers of the darkness of this world, against spiritual wickedness in high places.

Ephesians 6:12

The movie "Wonder Woman" (1) is a cinematic genius. Sitting in the movie theatre with the surround sound totally captivated me. Normally while watching movies I am nitpicking the bad acting, calling the punchline before it is revealed, and generally ruining any movie for whoever dares to watch with me. I am a non-stop verbal narrator thinking out loud, which usually irritates my best friend and family! However with this movie I was stunned into silence. Not only is the storyline excellent, the lighting, cinematography, editing and set design are some of the best I have seen in recent years. As a professional photographer and wannabe filmmaker, I could appreciate the artistry and nuances of every scene. But what really struck me was not just the technical mastery, but the story and the sense of identity and close bond between the women of the tribe. They were fully prepared to fight to the death to protect each other, their home and their land. Talk about fierce females! Walking out the movie theater both my daughters and I were pumped, we felt like we could kick down doors and take over the world! Yay for girl power.

In the real world we are fierce warrior women who have lost sight of our identity. We get beat up with every trial and tribulation we endure, take on guilt and shame, and end up wounded warriors. If we lose our sense of identity as daughters of the one true King, we have lost our strength. When we realize that we come from royalty, and are prepared to put in the training to become wonder women who stick tighter; we will become unstoppable!

Living in fear paralyzes potential, prevents progress, and punishes our peace. Our emotions hold us hostage with every mood and whim. We are tossed by the winds of change and end up whimpering waifs. Ugh not a pretty sight ladies, and definitely not a great leading lady role anyone wants to play. Let's face it feelings are fickle. One day we feel on top of the world, the next day we are down in the dumps. Oh and do not get me started about how our monthly cycles put us in PMS crazy town! Did somebody say roller coaster ride? We keep ourselves in the perpetual "one day when we" cycle forever promising ourselves we will change but we never do.

Have you ever asked yourself why you are afraid? Perhaps your mind brews over your fears that your child will repeat familiar patterns. Perhaps you are tired of being strong for everyone else and you just want peace and harmony in your home. Peace comes with a price and we have to fight for it by relying on God when we do not feel strong. Listen sweetie, you have work to do. God has ordained you for a purpose, do not let your season be the reason you give up before you even try. God is raising an army of strong, fierce, powerful, heartfelt, empowering women who are going to change the world; are you willing to be one of them?

We are suffering from spiritual identity theft because the devil ransacked our home and stole our inheritance from us! We need to slam those doors shut, put in security, and patrols the grounds to keep that punk off our property.

The Armour of God

Put on the full armour of God, so that you can make your stand against the devil's schemes.

We must understand that the conflict we are in is the battle of the ages. Each soul that falls in the battle, wounded and unable to stand up, is a victory to the kingdom of darkness. That is not a pretty sight! If you are a Christian you are automatically a soldier as soon as you were drafted into the army of God. Before any soldier goes into battle it is very important that they go through the proper training. Once they are trained they would never think to face their enemy without the proper equipment. Although we do not acquire machine guns or heavy battle armoury, we can still activate such armour in the Word of God.

Many Christians have battles everyday but despite the battles and wars, you can continue to survive and even thrive during raging conflicts when you are fully equipped. Every soldier is given an uniform when they enlist. We too are given everything we need to be clothed as a soldier: boots, hats, belts and a uniform. Our warfare cannot be perfectly sound unless we use every part of the armour of God that He readily gives us. God has given us very specific tools to equip us to be prepared for war so we come out unscathed. The armour of God covers five vital components to protect you and one component for you to launch a counter-attack. This "God Gear" is invisible to the naked eye and comes packaged with power and might. It is readily available for you to use on a daily basis, you just need to step up and wear it. You would not leave the house partly dressed or naked would you? So why leave yourself exposed spiritually?

Ephesians 6 :10-18 explains it...

10 Finally, be strong in the Lord and in his mighty power. 11 Put on the full armour of God, so that you can take your stand against the devil's schemes. 12 For our struggle is not against flesh and blood, but against the rulers, against the authorities, against the powers of this dark world and against the spiritual forces of evil in the heavenly realms. 13 Therefore put on the full armour of God, so that when the day of evil comes, you may be able to stand your ground, and after you have done everything, to stand. 14 Stand firm then, with the belt of truth buckled around your waist, with the breastplate of righteousness in place, 15 and with your feet fitted with the readiness that comes from the gospel of peace. 16 In addition to all this, take up the shield of faith, with which you can extinguish all the flaming arrows of the evil one. 17 Take the helmet of salvation and the sword of the Spirit, which is the word of God. 18 And pray in the Spirit on all occasions with all kinds of prayers and requests. With this in mind, be alert and always keep on praying for all the Lord's people.

The Helmet of Salvation:

The battle starts in our minds so it is super import to guard our minds with the helmet of salvation. This helps us to remember that all knowledge and understanding come from Christ. We are saved by God's grace and not by our works so keeping our thoughts founded on the Word of God is crucial.

Breastplate of Righteousness:

The breastplate strategically keeps our hearts pure and focused on God. This is crucial to protecting our feelings from getting hurt, to stop offense from setting in, and to keep our heart confident that we are the righteousness of Christ.

The Belt of Truth:

Believing the Truth of Jesus's death that He died for us on the cross is the divine exchange. This helps us stay girded with strength. Psalm 18:32 says... It is God that girds me with strength, and makes my way perfect.

The Shield of Faith:

Wielding our faith protects us from the fiery darts of the devil. When we have the faith in Jesus to protect us we can dispel the darkness.

The Sword of the Spirit:

This is the offensive component of the armour of God that puts us in the driving seat. Speaking God's Word out loud is us wielding the sword.

Repeating His promises helps us to believe what we hear. Wielding God's offensive weapon means that we do not have to be on the defensive the whole time. If you look at the concept of God's Word you will see it spells 'Sword'. God's Word = God Sword according to Lisa Bevere in her book "Girls with Swords". (2)

The Gospel of Peace:

Being ready to walk in peace and not be rattled by the battles that rage around you is key to enduring the storm. No matter what gets thrown at you when you know that wherever your feet shall tread you have the victory, you can wear those heels of peace with confidence.

One thing we have to watch out for are the cracks in our armour. These will open the doors to the devil to attack you. You counter attack this by praying the armour of God over your mind, body and soul on a daily basis; just like you would get dressed every day. Every morning while I am still laying in bed before my eyes open or my feet hit the floor, I immediately suit up with the armour of God so I can be fully prepared for my day ahead. Over the years I have taught my children to pray this too every morning and every night at bedtime so they are protected, and we even made up a song to help them remember it...

Prayer: Armour of God

Thank you God for the helmet of salvation, breastplate of righteousness, belt of truth, shield of faith, sword of the spirit, and the readiness of gospel of peace in Jesus name amen!

Expect Resistance

I am coming soon. Hold fast to what you have, so that no one may seize your crown.

Revelation 3:11

When you start advancing toward pursuing God's calling on your life and taking steps of obedience, the enemy does not like it. He may not know exactly what God has planned for you, but the heavenly protection surrounding you makes it evident that something special is going on. This is when we should arm ourselves with the weapons of warfare which include the knowledge that we WILL get resistance! In Steven Pressfield's book "The War of Art" (3) he talks about resistance as a common occurrence when we are pushing to do something outside our comfort zone.

Do you find when you decide to pursue something important then all of a sudden "all hell breaks loose"? All of a sudden the car breaks down, the appliances go on the blink, you get an overdue bill, the kids start acting up, you fight with your husband etc. When Jesus was anointed and came out the water the dove rested on Him as a sign of the Holy Spirit coming over Him. What we forget to realize is that directly afterwards he was taken into the wilderness and was tested! He had to endure forty days of belligerent harassment, no food, probably little sleep, emotional upheaval and many opportunities to question his calling. What I find fascinating is that the devil attacked Jesus on three particular areas: he questioned his calling, he questioned his trust in God, and he questioned his identity as the one true Christ. So in other words Satan tempted Jesus to give in, show off his pride, and to compromise on his beliefs by giving in. During the temptation did you notice that Jesus did not argue back, he did not try to defend himself, he did not try to convince the devil otherwise; he just said "it is written". Drop the mic people... He plain and simply stated the facts without the drama, emotional whoopsies or arguments. We should take a leaf out of Jesus's book and every time the enemy tries to tempt us to get angry, frustrated, sad, rejected; is to put him in his place and declare out loud that it is written!

Realize this: the harder the warfare the bigger the calling. If we can flip the script and realize that every time we experience hardships, we can rest assured it only means that we are on the right track to pursuing

God's plan for our lives. Nothing worth doing happens easily so keep the faith, dig in your heels and refuse to give in. It is just a matter of waiting out the storm, and while we are waiting it is super important we stay in peace, refuse to grumble and complain, and pursue praise. When we know we have already won the war, we just need to take a firm stance, put our hands on our hips, and with a bit of sass declare "I will NOT be moved back off devil!" You are a royal daughter of the King wearing a crown of beauty so hold your head up high darling so your crown does not fall off!

Here is another doozie, did not be surprised that after a victory you get tested once again. Resistance is a sign you are onto something big and the devil does not want you to gain ground, so hold your ground and push back. You are not a weak waif that needs to accept the attacks and bear the punishment, it is time to put on your big girl panties and fight like a girl!!!

Spiritual Attacks

Blessed be the LORD my strength which teaches my hands to war, and my fingers to fight.

Psalm 144:1

The Greek word "skotos" **(4)** means "darkness, either physical or moral" meaning the soul has lost its perceptive power. Satan attacks what God plans for good. When we are attacked and lose our perspective, we should look for the opposite of our attacks to see the positive outcome. If the enemy is attacking your ability to pray, then he is obviously trying to block you from hearing important instruction from God. Spiritual attacks come multi pronged: they attack your mind, body, emotions, and relationships usually at the same time. These dramatic events usually come in quick succession, and come to shipwreck your faith to get you discouraged so you forgot God's promises for your life. Be warned, the devil is after your destiny and assignment as a child of God! The great news is that we have a secret weapon.

John 16:33

I have told you these things, so that in me you may have peace. In this world you will have trouble. But take heart! I have overcome the world.

Author Ryan LeStrange writes in his book "Overcoming Spiritual Attack: Identify and Break Eight Common Symptoms" **(5)**, there are eight symptoms of a spiritual attack. They include a lack of spiritual passion, the feelings of extreme frustration, lacking peace, feeling sluggish and unusually tired, having a strong urge to give up, a sense of being drawn back to old habits and bondages, questioning the direction God has given you that once seemed clear.

Spiritual attacks cause heaviness and physical symptoms. These include tiredness, confusion, fear, sickness, weariness, hopelessness, loneliness, depression, confusion, anxiety, identity crisis, procrastination, doubt, anger outbursts, tension in relationships. None of these are positive and are designed to slow you down and put a heavy on you so you cannot take action. Attacks cause you to give up on your promises.

Once I decided to press through and seek God for an answer to my situation, the attacks were on. I clearly recall two incidents that found me waking in my bed wrestling with a demonic presence. I was fast asleep dreaming that an evil spirit was chasing me and I was running as fast as I could. The spirit grabbed me by the throat in my dream and I could feel its stranglehold constricting my throat. The next thing I knew I was waking up and realized it had pinned me down in my bed. My arms felt paralyzed beside me and I was tossing my head around trying to get free. All I could muster was "Jesus! Jesus! Jesus!". My frenzy caused enough of a commotion that it woke my husband lying next to me. He was calling to me to wake up as he was frightened by the demonstration. Once fully awake I explained the situation to him, we prayed together and it left. I discovered my throat felt parched and sore from all the screaming and fighting, a physical demonstration of a real spiritual battle. It happened once again but this time I was prepared and screamed "Jesus save me!" before it could grab my throat. I realized the power and authority the name of Jesus has. On a separate occasion I woke at 3am with a foreboding sense of fear and death in our house. I got up and checked on each of my children who were sleeping. I was breaking, binding and declaring the Word over my family while pacing the floor. I prayed the angels encamped around each of my family members and sealed the house with the blood of Jesus. Soon the demonic spirit left and the house was at peace.

Psalm 34:7

The angel of the Lord encamps around those who fear him, and he delivers them.

For two years I was confused about my purpose and the direction I should take. Clarity seemed fleeting. I prayed that God would show me what He wanted me to do, and all I would get was static noise with no peace. My body showed physical signs too with depression, tiredness, lack of hope and incessant crying. I have always been a glass overflowing kind of girl, so being sad and depressed was out of character. When there is sin or trauma in the soul the wounds give demonic powers the right to attack you. What I did not realize was the demonic attacks were continuing because I had not dealt with the soul wounds in my own heart. No matter how much praying, fasting, breaking and binding I did; it proved useless if the devil had a legal right to harass me. It had to start with me cleaning out the cobwebs of my soul so that my prayers would be effective and powerful.

Many Christians live defeated lives because they do not understand or believe in the spiritual world and how it affects our everyday lives. God gives us the tools to effectively do spiritual warfare so we can break free and claim the promises He has for us. This is where wielding the sword of the spirit, which is the Word of God, is our weapon of choice for breaking through. Praying out loud wielding the sword of the spirit quoting God's Word is sending lightening bolts of electricity into the spiritual world. It starts and ends with repentance so when in doubt repent! This immediately gets us into alignment with God and takes back any authority we might have unknowingly given to the devil to mess with us.

Prayer: Release from Spiritual Attacks

Dear Lord thank You for the power of the name of Jesus and the word of my testimony. I repent for all sin and transgressions in my soul that have allowed the enemy legal ground in my life. I cancel the plans and attacks of the enemy and send them back to hell. I seal my mind, body and soul with the blood of Jesus and pray the angels encamp around me and my family. Thank you for the Holy Spirit fire of protection that guards my heart and mind. In Jesus name amen!

Devil is a legalist

These are legal requirements for you to observe from generation to generation, wherever you may live.

Numbers 35:29

Have you ever felt like when you try to advance you hit your head against a glass ceiling, brick wall or stainless steel door? It is as if there are barricades and invisible barriers holding you back. This my friends, is a classic sign that you may have unwittingly given over the deeds to your dominion to the devil. Do not be fooled by the disguises. We are not going to give the enemy any more credit than he needs, but realize that the devil is a legalist and he knows his rights and will exercise them to the letter. If you give him legal ground to mess with your life he will. You will be left wondering why everything seems to fall apart no matter what you do. What we need to do is look at things with our eyes wide open. If we were sitting in a court of law there is a system to how one can be dragged into court. We are going to unravel the yarn of lies you might have been believing so you can look at the evidence held against you and defend your case and win! How you recognize the fake is by studying the original. The three markers that Identify The Holy Spirit are (a) He is God, (b) He is the servant of God who focuses on Jesus, (c) He is holy.

John 16:13–14

13 But when he, the Spirit of truth, comes, he will guide you into all the truth. He will not speak on his own; he will speak only what he hears, and he will tell you what is yet to come. 14 He will glorify me because it is from me that he will receive what he will make known to you.

We protect and safeguard ourselves by...

- Humbling Ourselves (1 Peter 5:5–6).
- Receiving the love of the Truth (2 Thessalonians 2:9–12).
- Cultivating the fear of the Lord (Proverbs 1:7).
- Keeping our focus on the cross (Galatians 6:14).

Understanding the Courts of Heaven

God stands up to open heaven's court. He pronounces judgment on the judges.

Psalm 82:1

It was during a time of prayer and seeking God to discover the cause of my own situation that God gave me a vision. It is a cold, grey and wet day and I am standing in a field thick with fog. I am wearing my battle gear looking very disheveled, my sword and shield appear buckled and bent hanging at my side. I am worn out from this fight. I cannot see more than two steps ahead of me. I can hear the taunting jeers of the enemy in the distance. I get into the battle stance wielded my sword around my head, but who am I kidding? One swipe and I will be on my face kissing the floor. I am tired, I am cold, and I am alone. All my yelling and screaming has worn me out and my voice is barely audible. I am dressed and ready for battle but my efforts are fruitless and getting me nowhere. I asked the Holy Spirit to reveal to me what this meant and quickly I heard "You are so busy wearing yourself out fighting on the battlefield, but that is not where the battle is won. Take it to the courts and Jesus will fight it for you." It never dawned on me what the concept of the courts of heaven actually are. Why are the courts so significant? I began my search and I came across a video by Robert Henderson called the "The Courts of Heaven" and it sunk into my spirit.

Robert Henderson author of "Unlocking destinies in the Courts of Heaven" (6) explains that we all have a book of life in heaven that has our destinies already written in it. God's plan for us is for us to be blessed and to walk in victory, but often the devil has access to our lives through sin and curses to wreak havoc. We have a unique God-ordained destiny that we were designed and fashioned for, but we often struggle to achieve this destiny.

Psalm 139:16 says,

Your eyes saw my unformed body; all the days ordained for me were written in your book before one of them came to be.

This confirms that there is a book in Heaven that contains the destiny planned for each of us, and yet many many people live their lives never fully realizing their destinies. This is due to the barriers, blockages and debilitations the devil throws at us to thwart God's plan for our lives. In doing an online search of the bible I found 61 results for the word "courts" (7) here are just a few which include; 1 Chronicles 28:12, 2 Chronicles 23:5 , 2 Chronicles 33:5, Psalm 65:4, Psalm 84:2, Psalm 84:10, Psalm 92:13, Psalm 96:8, Psalm 100:4, Psalm 116:19, Psalm 135:2.

For those of you who work in the legal system you may have a much better understanding of how the courts of law work in your country. Of course, every country is a little different, but the basics are the same. In the USA (8) the legal system is in part inherited from English common law and depends on an adversarial system of justice. In an adversarial system, litigants present their cases before a neutral party like a judge. The arguments presented by each litigant (represented by lawyers) allows the judge or jury to determine the truth about the dispute. Evidence and testimony are presented by lawyers to the court. In heaven God is our judge and He sits on the throne (like the Supreme Court) in the courts of heaven. Jesus is our lawyer and advocate who argues on our behalf and presents evidence.

Job 1 : 6-12 shows us this in action...

When the day came for the heavenly beings to appear before the Lord, Satan was there among them. The Lord asked him, "What have you been doing?" Satan answered, "I have been walking here and there, roaming around the earth." "Did you notice my servant Job?" the Lord asked. "There is no one on earth as faithful and good as he is. He worships me and is careful not to do anything evil." Satan replied, "Would Job worship you if he got nothing out of it? You have always protected him and his family and everything he owns. You bless everything he does, and you have given him enough cattle to fill the whole country. But now suppose you take away everything he has—he will curse you to your face!" "All right," the Lord said to Satan, "everything he has is in your power, but you must not hurt Job himself." So Satan left.

I have often pondered why Satan was allowed to be present before the Lord and get the chance to test Job. As the story goes, Job loses his family, his livestock and his whole homestead in one day. He is stripped of everything and gets sick. Even his closest friends start thinking it was something he did or some sin he committed that brought on the calamity. Yet, we know from the scriptures that it was not anything Job did, or any sin he committed. It was that Satan had brought an accusation against Job in the courts of heaven, and God granted Satan the right to mess with his life. If Job was really loved by God and God loved him, why would God allow him to go through that? Now I know, it sounds totally unfair, but God is a fair judge and a fair God.

Revelation 12:10 says...

Then I heard a loud voice in heaven say: "Now have come the salvation and the power and the kingdom of our God, and the authority of his Messiah. For the accuser of our brothers and sisters, who accuses them before our God day and night, has been hurled down.

Satan is constantly accusing believers and he is called the accuser of the brethren. He is looking for any excuse to bring you down to allow God's protection to be lifted up from around you, so that he can mess with you and go back to God and say, "You see! You destined her for a purpose but look she failed." The inherent problem is that most people are frustrated with their lives because they intuitively know that they were created for more in life, but what they have experienced does not reflect that. We are being stolen from and need to know how to go into the Courts of Heaven to reclaim and unlock our destinies by dissolving the curses and accusations placed against us. The devil cannot work in your life without access.

God as a fair judge has to make the judgements accordingly with the evidence He has before Him. Did you know that you have the right to appear in court? We have the right to defend ourselves and we can find legal ground in order to win the war. While God is the judge, we are the petitioners, Jesus is our advocate or mediator, the Holy Spirit is our witness, and Satan is the prosecutor. Many of us Christians fail to understand this concept, we think spiritual warfare means we gotta go out there and do a William Wallace screaming rebukes down the countryside lopping our enemies heads off. There is actually a far more effective method by going to the courts of heaven. Time to put on a stylish royal robe and take back our authority!

Isaiah 43:26

Review the past for me, let us argue the matter together; state the case for your innocence.

The courts of heaven have a protocol. Just like in the courts on earth, you can avoid going to court if you are able to settle the matter out of court. Author Doug Addison has a fabulous training called "Understanding the Courts of Heaven" (9) video series. Addison says "The Cross of Christ is our verdict that allows us to enter into the justice system of God. We still need to enforce the verdict of the Name and Blood of Jesus and battle our adversary. You operate in the Courts of Heaven through prayer and an intimate relationship with the Lord." There are 6 different types of courts: the courts of mediation (reconciliation), Court of Petition, the Throne of Grace, the Court of Mount Zion, the Court of the Accuser, the Court of the Ancient of Days (Supreme Court). (10)

Romans 8:2

Because through Christ Jesus the law of the Spirit who gives life has set you free from the law of sin and death.

We start by approaching God with thanksgiving and praise, then we can enter the gates of the courts. Once we are in the gates, we want to discover what Satan is accusing us of, so that we can defend ourselves. Jesus is our ultimate defender, He is our advocate who will stand up and mediate for us. That is why we plead the blood of Jesus over ourselves. We plead in Jesus' name because we are not there on our own authority. We do not have a leg to stand on. We are products of our sinful nature, we are born into sin, but when we take on God's nature and Jesus' nature, we are transformed. Just imagine Jesus giving you this beautiful red robe of the blood of Jesus and clothing you in royalty, putting a crown on your head so you can come forward in the courts. Jesus is standing right beside you testifying on your behalf that even though Satan is accusing you, Jesus can say that you are covered. If Satan has any dirt on you, like anything hidden in your closet such as unforgiven sins, he will use any evidence he can to bring down your case.

God often gets a bad rap and gets blamed for injustices in the world. God is a just God and He honours the protocol of the spiritual realm just like we obey the rules of our society. The great news is that we can put in a claim to get repaid for the losses and things the enemy has stolen from us by using the system of the courts of heaven and following heaven's protocol.

Matthew 7:7

"Ask and it will be given to you; seek and you will find; knock and the door will be opened to you."

Job had everything stripped from him and after his friends started questioning if his calamities were his own fault, he did not get angry and argue with them. Instead, he prayed for his friends because he knew they meant well because they did not understand the full picture. The legal system is one of checks and balances and just like a court of law it has specific ways of working. If we want the verdict to swing in our favour we have to remain blameless, this means not agreeing with the accusing party the devil. If he can tempt us to sin by getting us angry, blaming God or people, then he can use that incriminating evidence against us. That way our verdict gets held up and we do not get our answer. The devil will try his best to tempt us and cause us to slip so when we come before the courtroom he hurls accusatory "evidence" against us. God wants to judge the situation in our favour, so the key is to stop agreeing with the devil as you are just playing into his hands! It can be tempting to want to give into revenge, anger and bitterness; but keep your slate clean by walking in forgiveness and reminding yourself daily to forgive others. Remind the enemy that you are washed and forgiven by the blood so he cannot blame you.

Romans 12:19

Do not take revenge, my dear friends, but leave room for God's wrath, for it is written: "It is mine to avenge; I will repay," says the Lord.

Once Job passed his test by remaining faithful to the Lord, he received his repayment in double portion of what he had originally lost. We need to put in a claim in the courts to get repaid but first we have to come to the courts blameless and without prejudice.

Job 42:10, 12a (NKJV)

And the Lord restored Job's losses when he prayed for his friends. Indeed the Lord gave Job twice as much as he had before ... Now the Lord blessed the latter days of Job more than his beginning.

I like to think of it as a good thing when I get persecuted because I know it means that I am due for an upgrade in my circumstances. Something good is going to happen just around the corner if I can just hold on through the wild ride!

Standing in the Gap

I looked for a man among them who would build up the wall and stand before me in the gap on behalf of the land so I would not have to destroy it, but I found none.

Ezekiel 22:30

Standing in the gap is a form of intercessory prayer where we bridge the gap between God and the people who are far from Him and His presence. When we stand in the gap in prayer, we can pray for God's help, mercy, intervention and forgiveness on the behalf of individuals, groups of people or nations. This is how we pray for others in need or who are unable or unwilling to pray for themselves. We have parental rights to pray over our children and protect them. We also have the right to pray and ask for forgiveness on their behalf when they cannot do so themselves by standing in the gap. This means that although they might not be old enough or willing to acknowledge their need for repentance, we can do that for them since we are their guardians.

There are several kinds of situations where you might feel led to stand in the gap for someone and pray on their behalf. Praying for someone going through a crisis who does not know how to pray, praying for someone in rebellion to God, praying corporately for nations and communities, praying against injustice, praying for those who do not believe in God, praying against corruption, praying for the weak and sick who may not be able to pray for themselves, praying for those experiencing stress who do not have the energy or know-how, praying in agreement with God's will for an individual or country.

The key is to follow the protocol of entering the courts of heaven beginning with thanksgiving, praise and repentance. Only then can we make our petitions known to God. It starts with humbling ourselves and this means there is no room for pride. We have to walk in repentance and turn away from old behaviours and bad ways of thinking. When we pray we do so in accordance with the Word, not our soulish or selfish prayers (so keep your complaints to yourself). We press through by seeking God which means studying the scriptures, waiting on God and being patient.

A good way to start is to write down your petition or what answer you are seeking from God. Look up corresponding scriptures where God has answered prayers in the past about your situation. If you do not find an exact match do not worry about it, you are looking for instances where God shows His faithfulness and makes good on His promises. You would write down the scripture and use it as your "evidence" when petitioning for your case. For an example, praying for an unsaved loved one you would find scriptures where God saves His people and does not wish for anyone to perish such as;

2 Peter 3:9

The Lord is not slack concerning his promise, as some men count slackness; but is long-suffering to us, not willing that any should perish, but that all should come to repentance.

Your prayer would go something like this...

Prayer: Standing in the Gap

Dear Lord I thank You for saving me and accepting me as your child. I praise You for all the blessings you've given me in my life. I repent Lord of all sin that I have committed (both knowingly and unknowingly) and ask for your forgiveness. I come before you with a humble heart. Lord I stand in the gap for my loved one _____ (insert name) and I ask that you show mercy to him/her and save them by bringing them into your Kingdom (or mention what answer you seek). I ask this in accordance to your Word in 2 Peter 3:9 "The Lord is not slack concerning his promise, as some men count slackness; but is long-suffering to us, not willing that any should perish, but that all should come to repentance." Thank you in Jesus name amen!

Repentance is the Key

It was also written that this message would be proclaimed in the authority of his name to all the nations, beginning in Jerusalem: 'There is forgiveness of sins for all who repent.'

Luke 24:47

Repentance stops the devil using ammunition to accuse us in the courts of heaven. He accuses us of sins and transgressions and if he has evidence against us, he can block the blessings of God in our lives. The big deal is that when we walk in repentance, he can try to accuse us, but all he sees is Jesus who is our advocate and our covering. The steps to walking out your breakthrough is to come before the Lord in humility, repent for your sins, ask for forgiveness and adopt a new way of thinking. Ask God what He wants you to learn from your mistakes and He will gladly show you. Do not go around the mountain again and again repeating the same mistakes because you will keep taking the test until you pass.

Ephesians 5 : 6-14

Let no one deceive you with empty words, for because of such things God's wrath comes on those who are disobedient. Therefore do not be partners with them. For you were once darkness, but now you are light in the Lord. Live as children of light (for the fruit of the light consists in all goodness, righteousness and truth) and find out what pleases the

Lord. Have nothing to do with the fruitless deeds of darkness, but rather expose them. It is shameful even to mention what the disobedient do in secret. But everything exposed by the light becomes visible—and everything that is illuminated becomes a light. This is why it is said; "Wake up, sleeper, rise from the dead, and Christ will shine on you."

God knew what we needed long before we knew we needed it, and He provides this daily bread in the form of The Lord's Prayer.

Matthew 6 : 5-13

5 And when you pray, do not be like the hypocrites, for they love to pray standing in the synagogues and on the street corners to be seen by others. Truly I tell you, they have received their reward in full. 6 But when you pray, go into your room, close the door and pray to your Father, who is unseen. Then your Father, who sees what is done in secret, will reward you. 7 And when you pray, do not keep on babbling like pagans, for they think they will be heard because of their many words. 8 Do not be like them, for your Father knows what you need before you ask him. This, then, is how you should pray: "'Our Father in heaven, hallowed be your name, 10 your kingdom come, your will be done, on earth as it is in heaven. 11 Give us today our daily bread. 12 And forgive us our debts, as we also have forgiven our debtors. 13 And lead us not into temptation, but deliver us from the evil one.[14 For if you forgive other people when they sin against you, your heavenly Father will also forgive you. 15 But if you do not forgive others their sins, your Father will not forgive your sins.

Another important step is to censor your senses (your eyes, ears, and mouth). Garbage in equals garbage out. Saturate yourself in the new routine of asking for forgiveness on a daily basis and soon it will become spiritual habit and you will develop muscle memory.

Fasting & Praying

I ate no choice food; no meat or wine touched my lips; and I used no lotions at all until the three weeks were over.

Daniel 10:3

Jesus fasted for fourty days in the wilderness, no food or water and persistent harassment from the devil. Every time He was tempted Jesus quoted the Word "it is written". Fasting brings our flesh into alignment with our spirit. When we crucify the flesh by not giving it what it wants, we are redirecting our focus on the Lord. There are several examples of effective fasting in the bible; like when Esther fasted for three days on behalf of her Jewish nation before she brought her request to the King.

Esther 4 :10-11, 15-16

10 Then she instructed him to say to Mordecai, 11 "All the king's officials and the people of the royal provinces know that for any man or woman who approaches the king in the inner court without being summoned the king has but one law: that they be put to death unless the king extends the gold scepter to them and spares their lives. But thirty days have passed since I was called to go to the king." 15 Then Esther sent this reply to Mordecai: 16 "Go, gather together all the Jews who are in Susa, and fast for me. Do not eat or drink for three days, night or day. I and my attendants will fast as you do. When this is done, I will go to the king, even though it is against the law. And if I perish, I perish."

Esther knew she was risking certain death if she approached the King without being summoned. By approaching God first, she was humbling herself and her nation so that the king's heart would be softened and open to hearing her request. Can you imagine if she went in guns blazing having a hissy fit, yelling and accusing Haman of being a traitor? She would have probably had three seconds before the guards would have acted swiftly and off with her head! Fasting makes us humble and helps us push through our situation with fervent prayer. Fasting removes pride which God detests, because it keeps us from acknowledging our need for a saviour.

1 Peter 5:5–6

5 In the same way, you who are younger, submit yourselves to your elders. All of you, clothe yourselves with humility toward one another, because, "God opposes the proud but shows favour to the humble." 6 Humble yourselves, therefore, under God's mighty hand, that he may lift you up in due time.

We see the effectiveness of fasting in the story of Daniel. When he is captured by the Babylonians and forced into training to become a servant for the king, he requests a fast.

Daniel 1: 8-16...

8 But Daniel resolved not to defile himself with the royal food and wine, and he asked the chief official for permission not to defile himself this way. 9 Now God had caused the official to show favour and compassion to Daniel, 10 but the official told Daniel, "I am afraid of my lord the king, who has assigned your food and drink. Why should he see you looking worse than the other young men your age? The king would then have my head because of you." 11 Daniel then said to the guard whom the chief official had appointed over Daniel, Hananiah, Mishael and Azariah, 12 "Please test your servants for ten days: Give us nothing but vegetables to eat and water to drink. 13 Then compare our appearance with that of the young men who eat the royal food, and treat your servants in accordance with what you see." 14 So he agreed to this and tested them for ten days. 15 At the end of the ten days they looked healthier and better nourished than any of the young men who ate the royal food. 16 So the guard took away their choice food and the wine they were to drink and gave them vegetables instead.

When Daniel is in the king's service, he once again turns to fasting when he is seeking revelation and understanding about a troubling dream.

Daniel 10: 1-14 says...

1In the third year of Cyrus king of Persia, a revelation was given to Daniel (who was called Belteshazzar). Its message was true and it concerned a great war. The understanding of the message came to him in a vision. 2 At that time I, Daniel, mourned for three weeks. 3 I ate no choice food; no meat or wine touched my lips; and I used no lotions at all until the three weeks were over. 4 On the twenty-fourth day of the first month, as I was standing on the bank of the great river, the Tigris, 5 I looked up and there before me was a man dressed in linen, with a belt of fine gold from Uphaz around his waist. 6 His body was like topaz, his face like lightning, his eyes like flaming torches, his arms and legs like the gleam of burnished bronze, and his voice like the sound of a multitude. 7 I, Daniel, was the only one who saw the vision; those who were with me did not see it, but such terror overwhelmed them that they fled and hid themselves. 8 So I was left alone, gazing at this great vision; I had no strength left, my face turned deathly pale and I was helpless. 9 Then I heard him speaking, and as I listened to him, I fell into a deep sleep, my face to the ground. 10 A hand touched me and set me trembling on my hands and knees. 11 He said, "Daniel, you who are highly esteemed, consider carefully the words I am about to speak to you, and stand up, for I have now been sent to you." And when he said this to me, I stood up trembling. 12 Then he continued, "Do not be afraid, Daniel. Since the first day that you set your mind to gain understanding and to humble yourself before your God, your words were heard, and I have come in response to them. 13 But the prince of the Persian kingdom resisted me twenty-one days. Then Michael, one of the chief princes, came to help me, because I was detained there with the king of Persia. 14 Now I have come to explain to you what will happen to your people in the future, for the vision concerns a time yet to come."

If you notice that in this instance Daniel persisted with his fast until he received an answer to his prayer. For three weeks he humbled himself, fasted and prayed. The angel says that on the first day his request was granted but that the Prince of Persia (a demonic stronghold) resisted the angel from delivering the answer to Daniel. Sometimes we have to be persistent enough to push through to get our answer. Often times the demonic forces in the spiritual realm are resisting us getting our break through so it is important that we do not give up!

This is the kind of fast I personally felt led to do for my own situation. I sensed that there was a breakthrough coming but there was incredible resistance to us receiving the manifestation of our promise. My husband and I enlisted the prayer support of our family and chose to undertake a seven day Daniel fast (11) that consisted of eating just fruit, vegetables and water. No sugar, meat, caffeine, carbs etc. Wowza what a challenge! To be honest it was hard; the caffeine withdrawal headaches were brutal, the sluggishness and lack of energy was frustrating but we knew the outcome would be worthwhile. We undertook praying every time we had a hunger pang, and instead of grumbling and complaining we did not tell anyone but a select few. This kept us accountable to complete the fast and humble enough to stay focused. The best part was that we did our fast one week before Thanksgiving so we had a great reason to feast and celebrate once we were done!

If you have a pressing issue that you know needs persistence and prayer, I invite you to consider taking up a fast. Mostly it is done as seven to ten days eating only vegetables and drinking water or smoothies. Do not think of it as a rigid set of rules, just do it for however long you feel led to do it. It may just be enough to fast for a day so ask the Lord in prayer what He advises you do. How you prepare is before you begin the fast start eating lightly, cut down on caffeine and sugar (to reduce those horrid caffeine headaches), and try cutting back on heavy fatty foods. Remember every hunger pang is like an alarm reminder for you to focus and pray. This shows the devil that you mean business. Keep yourself covered in prayer and ideally fast in pairs or in groups for spiritual and moral support.

Matthew 18:20

For where two or three gather in my name, there am I with them.

Curses

This day I call the heavens and the earth as witnesses against you that I have set before you life and death, blessings and curses. Now choose life, so that you and your children may live.

Deuteronomy 30:9

Curses are vehicles of supernatural power. We have the power to bless or curse with our thoughts, words and actions. The big lie the devil wants us to believe is that the demonic realm and curses do not exist. Staying in the dark prevents us from claiming our rights as adopted sons and daughters of God. Do not agree with the demonic, take back control and exercise your rights. God's Word is clear;

Ephesians 6:12

For our struggle is not against flesh and blood, but against the rulers, against the authorities, against the powers of this dark world and against the spiritual forces of evil in the heavenly realms.

How do curses work and why do they exist? There are many root causes of curses and we will cover some of them to give you an idea of how you may be unknowingly opening the door to allow curses to operate in your life. The two primary reasons are not listening to God's voice (disobedience) and idolatry (false gods). For a more in depth study I recommend reading "Blessing or Curse: You can Choose" by Derek Prince. **(12)**

According to Derek Prince he explains that there are seven indications of a curse:

1) Mental and/or emotional breakdown.

2) Repeated or chronic sickness (especially hereditary illnesses).

3) Barrenness and miscarriage or female related problems.

4) Breakdown of marriage and family alienation (breakdown of relationships).

5) Continuing financial insufficiency (constant financial problems).

6) Being accident prone.

7) History of suicide, unnatural or early deaths.

Deuteronomy 27: 15-26 explains tips of curses:

15 "Cursed is anyone who makes an idol—a thing detestable to the Lord, the work of skilled hands—and sets it up in secret." Then all the people shall say, "Amen!" 16 "Cursed is anyone who dishonors their father or mother." Then all the people shall say, "Amen!" 17 "Cursed is anyone who moves their neighbor's boundary stone." Then all the people shall say, "Amen!" 18 "Cursed is anyone who leads the blind astray on the road." Then all the people shall say, "Amen!" 19 "Cursed is anyone who withholds justice from the foreigner, the fatherless or the widow." Then all the people shall say, "Amen!" 20 "Cursed is anyone who sleeps with his father's wife, for he dishonors his father's bed." Then all the people shall say, "Amen!" 21 "Cursed is anyone who has sexual relations with any animal." Then all the people shall say, "Amen!" 22 "Cursed is anyone who sleeps with his sister, the daughter of his father or the daughter of his mother." Then all the people shall say, "Amen!" 23 "Cursed is anyone who sleeps with his mother-in-law." Then all the people shall say, "Amen!" 24 "Cursed is anyone who kills their neighbor secretly." Then all the people shall say, "Amen!" 25 "Cursed is anyone who accepts a bribe to kill an innocent person." Then all the people shall say, "Amen!" 26 "Cursed is anyone who does not uphold the words of this law by carrying them out." Then all the people shall say, "Amen!"

(1) Curses from Disobedience

Common forms of God's judgment toward disobedient people or

nations is to pronounce a curse on them. Failure to honour our father and mother is the first commandment with a promise. Any disrespect for parents and subsequent rebellion, fear, rejection and hatred opens us to a curse.

Ephesians 6:1

Children, obey your parents in the Lord, for this is right. 2 "Honor your father and mother"—which is the first commandment with a promise-3 "so that it may go well with you and that you may enjoy long life on the earth.

Samuel 15:23

For rebellion is like the sin of divination, and arrogance like the evil of idolatry. Because you have rejected the word of the Lord, he has rejected you as king."

(2) Curses from Idolatry and Abominations

God is clear that we are not to have any other gods before Him. Idolatry is making an idol of anything or anyone that excludes our reliance on God. This includes seeking advice through fortune tellers, ouija board, tarot cards, horoscopes, occult practices, foreign gods and religions (Buddhism, Hinduism, Humanism, New Age, Scientology, Mysticism or Muslim etc.). Idolatry also includes the love of money, materialism, accolades, approval from people, addiction to drugs or nicotine, gluttony, pornography, gambling, sex, or anything that takes your focus and time away from your faith in God. Having another god besides the one true God includes every form of occult practice. The curse from the occult affects up the fourth and fifth generation, so you may be suffering the effects of a curse your long lost relative did back in the day.

Exodus 23:24-26

24 Do not bow down before their gods or worship them or follow their practices. You must demolish them and break their sacred stones to pieces. 25 Worship the Lord your God, and his blessing will be on your food and water. I will take away sickness from among you, 26 and none will miscarry or be barren in your land. I will give you a full life span.

(3) Curses from Witchcraft, Divination and Occult Activity

When you bring anything that is associated with witchcraft or the occult into your home, you are opening the way for a curse to come into your life. The item that is associated with or has been involved in an occult activity is considered a transference object, and gives Satan the right of access. You need to go through your house from top to bottom, clean out anything that is associated with the occult and burn them (even if they are antique family heirlooms). These include any kind of superstitious items that are supposed to bring good luck like a horseshoe, lucky charm or dream catcher etc. It does not ward off bad luck but in fact opens the door for Satan.

Occult involvement includes: fortune-telling, ouija board, horoscopes, superstition, rock/metal/death metal music, drugs, eastern religions, African artifacts, board games (Ouija board, dungeons and dragons), books about new age or other religions etc. Visiting a fortune teller can block your ability to speak in tongues, affect your mind, and mess with your peace.

Deuteronomy 7:26

Do not bring a detestable thing into your house or you, like it, will be set apart for destruction. Regard it as vile and utterly detest it, for it is set apart for destruction.

Witch doctors, spiritists and diviners are particularly detestable to God. Their use of demonic incantations and spells are word curses pronounced over people. An ancestor who sought dark forces (like other gods) in the form of a fortune teller, clairvoyant, spiritist, scientologist is witchcraft. Even if it was done "just for fun" or with no serious intent, the devil takes it very seriously and will exercise his rights to destroy you with a curse. Witchcraft uses manipulation and control with practices like divination as a form of predictive ability.

See also Galatians 3:1, Numbers 22:6, Acts 16:16.

Rebellion (against God and authority figures) is as the sin of witchcraft and brings with it curses. Rejection can either be passive (poor self esteem, self-loathing), or aggressive (resentment, hatred, indifference).

1 Samuel 15:23

For rebellion is like the sin of divination, and arrogance like the evil of idolatry. Because you have rejected the word of the LORD, he has rejected you as king.

(4) Generational Curses

Sins of the father are passed down to the fourth and fifth generation. Examples of generational curses can include the breakup of the family (divorce), addiction (alcohol, drugs), abuse (molestation, incest, rape), early death (suicide, unexplained illness), serious and chronic illness (cancer, arthritis, Parkinson's, Fibromyalgia), barrenness (infertility), financial insufficiency (poverty) etc. Usually these curses can be identified by their persistent and systematic appearances through many generations e.g. father, grandfather and great-grandfather died of heart attacks. The good news is that we can repent on behalf of our blood relatives and break and bind their effects.

Exodus 24 : 6-7

6 Moses took half of the blood and put it in basins, and the other half of the blood he sprinkled on the altar. 7 Then he took the book of the covenant and read it in the hearing of the people; and they said, "All that the LORD has spoken we will do, and we will be obedient!" 8 So Moses took the blood and sprinkled it on the people, and said, "Behold the blood of the covenant, which the LORD has made with you in accordance with all these words."

Jeremiah 32:18

You show love to thousands but bring the punishment for the parents' sins into the laps of their children after them.

(5) Word Curses

There is power of life and death in the tongue and we can either bless or curse others and ourselves with our words. If you have made a negative remark about yourself, if you have imposed something negative on yourself, you need to revoke it by speaking the positive. God's promises are voice activated, speak the Sword of the Spirit out loud. Repent of curses spoken over yourself and cancel their effects.

James 3:9

With the tongue we praise our Lord and Father, and with it we curse human beings, who have been made in God's likeness.

See also Exodus 22:28, Joshua 6:26 , Genesis 31:29-30, Psalm 118:17.

Stop agreeing with the enemy by saying things like: "It's driving me crazy!", "I love you to death", "I just can't take it anymore", "I'm sick and tired", "It runs in the family", "If there's a bug I'm the one to catch it", "I don't think I'll ever get pregnant again", "We've always fought like cats and dogs" , "I can't afford that", "I don't want this baby now", "It always happen to me", "I'm so clumsy", "I knew there was trouble", "Over my dead body", "What's the use of living", "I'd rather die than...", "I'm too poor to afford that" etc. Speak blessings over yourself by infusing positive words into your life.

(6) Curses from Treachery and Apostasy

Treachery is defined as a "violation of allegiance or of faith and confidence, an act of perfidy or treason"**(13)**. God is clear that those that reward evil for good for their own selfish way will in fact bring evil upon himself. Apostasy is "an act of refusing to continue to follow, obey, or recognize a religious faith" **(14)**. When a person turns his/her back on God and their faith, it is considered treachery and in return they bring a curse upon themselves.

Isaiah 59: 12-13

12 For our transgressions are multiplied before You, And our sins testify against us; For our transgressions are with us, And we know our iniquities: 13 Transgressing and denying the LORD, And turning away from our God, Speaking oppression and revolt, Conceiving in and uttering from the heart lying words.

See also Ezekiel 18:24, Lamentations 3: 64-66.

(7) Curses from Works of the flesh and Trusting in Man

We invite curses into our lives when we put our trust in our own works and efforts, and in the strength of man. This says to God we do not trust Him or need Him. In our own arrogance we elevate ourselves above God because we are showing that we trust ourselves more than we trust in God's divine providence, power and strength.

Jeremiah 17:5–6

5 This is what the Lord says: "Cursed is the one who trusts in man, who draws strength from mere flesh and whose heart turns away from the Lord. 6 That person will be like a bush in the wastelands; they will not see prosperity when it comes. They will dwell in the parched places of the desert, in a salt land where no one lives.

(8) Curses from Unscriptural Covenants

Unscriptural covenants include verbal and written agreements with people, groups and institutions that do not have a Godly foundation that require secrecy and pledges. In particular, Freemasonry has long been associated with marked curses and afflictions. If this group of people have false gods and you make a covenant with those people, you are also making a covenant with their gods. God is clear that idolatry will bring curses. When a person becomes a mason they have to pronounce self-imposed curses on themselves if they ever disclose the secrets of the masons. These curses include agreeing to having their tongue cut out, their right arm cut off, and their body exposed. Freemasonry is an idol religion and affects the entire family, the descendants, the spouse, and all the relatives. It has been speculated that freemasonry curses affect in particular the female line, which includes a wife, sister or daughter suffering from breast cancer or ovarian cancer (organs of fertility).

Exodus 20:5

You shall not bow down to them or serve them, for I the Lord your God am a jealous God, visiting the iniquity of the fathers on the children to the third and the fourth generation of those who hate me.

See also Exodus 23:32, 1 Samuel 18:1.

(9) Curses from Sexual Immorality

Did you have an abusive boyfriend who is a bad influence that just will not go away? Does it seem like his drama and destruction follow you? Blood covenants through pre marital sex or through pacts made with another through shedding of blood can bring curses. Sexual immorality includes fornication (sex outside of marriage), adultery, sexual abuse, rape, molestation, incest. Trauma, shock and abuse will open a person up to demonic interference and invite curses. The good news is that we can break off the soul ties and sever the curses through the blood of Jesus who is our ultimate blood sacrifice.

1 Corinthians 6:16

Or do you not know that he who is joined to a prostitute becomes one body with her? For, as it is written, "The two will become one flesh.

1 Corinthians 6:18

Flee from sexual immorality. Every other sin a person commits is outside the body, but the sexually immoral person sins against his own body.

(10) Curses from Injustice toward the helpless

Abortion is considered an injustice toward the helpless and is a detestable practice in God's eyes. Sacrificing one's own children on the altar of Baal or by putting them through the fire was a common occurrence in era of Judah. Abortion is murder and brings with it judgement and the curse of death.

Jeremiah 32:34-35

34 "But they put their detestable things in the house which is called by My name, to defile it. They built high places for Baal in the Valley of Ben Hinnom to sacrifice their sons and daughters to Molek, though I never commanded–nor did it enter my mind–that they should do such a detestable thing and so make Judah sin.

See also Leviticus 20:2, James 2:11, Romans 13:9, Matthew 5:21, Deuteronomy 5:17.

(11) Curses from Anti-Semitism

Nations and people who came against God's chosen people bring a curse upon themselves. Anyone who speaks badly of the Jewish nation is unknowingly invoking a curse upon themselves and opening the door to destruction.

Genesis 12:3

I will bless those who bless you, and whoever curses you I will curse; and all peoples on earth will be blessed through you."

Genesis 27:29

May nations serve you and peoples bow down to you. Be lord over your brothers, and may the sons of your mother bow down to you. May those who curse you be cursed and those who bless you be blessed.

(12) Curses from Withholding Tithes and Robbing God

Stinginess toward God brings a curse. The principle of what you sow you reap is evident here. Withholding what is rightfully God's brings a curse, often in the form of a lack of financial resources.

Malachi 3:8–10

8 "Will a mere mortal rob God? Yet you rob me. "But you ask, 'How are we robbing you?' "In tithes and offerings. 9 You are under a curse—your whole nation—because you are robbing me. 10 Bring the whole tithe into the storehouse, that there may be food in my house. Test me in this," says the Lord Almighty, "and see if I will not throw open the floodgates of heaven and pour out so much blessing that there will not be room enough to store it.

Malachi 3: 9-10

9 You are under a curse—your whole nation—because you are robbing me. 10 Bring the whole tithe into the storehouse, that there may be food in my house. Test me in this," says the Lord Almighty, "and see if I will not throw open the floodgates of heaven and pour out so much blessing that there will not be room enough to store it.

(13) Curses from Preaching False Doctrine

The Greek word "anathema" which has been taken over into the English language means "a votive offering, a thing devoted to God; a curse, the thing cursed" **(15)**. The dictionary defines 'anathema' as "one that is cursed by ecclesiastical authority, someone or something intensely disliked or loathed, usually used as a predicate nominative, a ban or curse solemnly, accompanied by excommunication" **(16)**. It is something so totally abhorrent to God that He will totally shut it off from Him and excommunicate his association. God detests false preaching and will 'anathema' or excommunicate those who speak falsely about His Word.

Galatians 1:6–9

6 I am astonished that you are so quickly deserting the one who called you to live in the grace of Christ and are turning to a different gospel— 7 which is really no gospel at all. Evidently some people are throwing you into confusion and are trying to pervert the gospel of Christ. 8 But even if we or an angel from heaven should preach a gospel other than the one we preached to you, let them be under God's curse! 9 As we have already said, so now I say again: If anybody is preaching to you a gospel other than what you accepted, let them be under God's curse!

(14) Curses from Theft and Perjury

Theft is not only a felony but also brings a curse upon those who commit this sin. Speaking falsely is perjury and also brings a curse.

Zechariah 5:3

And he said to me, "This is the curse that is going out over the whole land; for according to what it says on one side, every thief will be banished, and according to what it says on the other, everyone who swears falsely will be banished. 4 The Lord Almighty declares, 'I will send it out, and it will enter the house of the thief and the house of anyone who swears falsely by my name. It will remain in that house and destroy it completely, both its timbers and its stones.'

HOW TO BREAK FREE FROM CURSES

We release ourselves from the consequences of curses by confessing them as a sin. By repenting, obeying God, cleansing our lives and homes, and anointing our space brings us back into alignment and under God's protection.

Step 1 Repent:

Do not have anything in common with the devil to allow him to lay claim to you, to walk in true power we need to cleanse ourselves of all sin through repentance. Repent of all known doorways that you have opened to curses.

Step 2 Obey:

The key to receiving God's blessings is to obey God's voice. If you feel He is telling you to get rid of any offensive item, or apologize to someone, just do it.

The blessings we can expect for Obedience (according to Deuteronomy 28:1-14)

If you fully obey the Lord your God and carefully follow all His commands He promises to:

- Set you high above all the nations on earth.
- Bless you in the city and bless you in the country.
- Make you abundantly prosperous: your womb will be blessed, the crops of your land and the young of your livestock will multiply.
- Your basket and your kneading trough will be blessed.
- You will be blessed when you come in and blessed when you go out.

- Your enemies who rise up against you will be defeated before you. They will come at you from one direction but flee from you in seven.
- Your barns will be blessed and everything you put your hand to will be blessed. God will bless you in the land he is giving you.
- God will establish you as His holy people and all the peoples on earth will see that you are called by the name of the Lord, and they will fear you.
- God will open the heavens, the storehouse of his bounty, to send rain on your land in season and to bless all the work of your hands.
- You will lend to many nations but will borrow from none.
- The Lord will make you the head, not the tail. You will always be at the top, never at the bottom.

Step 3 Cleanse:

You need to close any open doors where you have given the devil legal right to enter your life and home. Cleanse your house by destroying all occult objects by destroying them in fire (such as on a barbecue) e.g. horoscope books, buddha idols, African art, eastern religious relics, lucky horse shoe, dream catcher, ouija board, tarot cards, wishing tree, mythical creatures, Asian art and artifacts (like dragons) etc. Ask the Holy Spirit to show you and He will. Burn them with fire and revoke their demonic hold.

Deuteronomy 7:25-26

After you conquer a nation, burn their idols. Don't get trapped into wanting the silver or gold on an idol. Even the metal on an idol is disgusting to the Lord, so destroy it. If you bring it home with you, both you and your house will be destroyed. Stay away from those disgusting idols!

Step 4 Anoint:

Once you have removed all offending items you need to anoint your home with oil. You can use something simple like olive oil and anoint every door post and window with the oil. Pray protection and the blood of Jesus over every member of the family and your home.

Prayer: Release from Curses

Consider writing down the topics that you feel convicted about, and feel free to omit those that don't apply. When you are done I suggest you take communion.

Dear Lord thank you for redeeming me from death by the sacrifice of Jesus's death on the cross and the dunamis resurrection power that lives in me. I repent for opening the doors to curses in my life. I break and cancel every effect from the curses of treachery, apostasy, disobedience, works of the flesh, trusting in man. I cancel every word curse I have spoken over myself and others, I break all generational curses in my bloodline right back to Adam. I cancel and break all unscriptural covenants, all effects of witchcraft, divination, fortune telling and all occult involvement by my own actions and those of my bloodline. I repent of idolatry and break curses brought on by making an idol out of anyone or anything other than God. I repent from bringing into my home any items that are an abomination and detestable to you Lord, I break the curses associated with these items. I cancel and break all soul ties to other people created through sexual immorality and blood covenants. I break all curses created through sexual immoral acts of fornication, adultery, perversion, pornography. I repent of the act or abortion and murder and cancel the curse of death over myself and my bloodline. I repent for my words and actions of anti-semitism and break the effects of the curse. I repent for robbing You God from tithes and cancel the curse of poverty over my finances. I repent for believing and speaking false doctrine and cancel its effects. I repent for my acts of theft and stealing from the innocent. I repent for acts of perjury ad speaking lies. I cancel, break and bind every curse in my life, in the lives of my immediate family and all future generations in my blood line. Thank you

Jesus for saving me and redeeming my life. I claim God's blessings and abundance as my inheritance as a child of God. In Jesus name amen!

Deliverance

But Moses told the people, "Don't be afraid. Just stand still and watch the LORD rescue you today. The Egyptians you see today will never be seen again.

Exodus 14:13

The first impact of Jesus's public ministry was that he was known as man who cast out evil spirits. People flocked to hear Him minister because they heard that He could heal them from their infirmities. A notable miracle Jesus performed was to cast out an evil spirit from a man. The evil spirit knew immediately who Jesus was before any of the disciples had a grasp of whose company they were in. There are two accounts of this incidence documented by Mark and Luke.

Mark 1 :21-28

21 Jesus and his disciples went to the town of Capernaum. Then on the next Sabbath he went into the Jewish meeting place and started teaching. 22 Everyone was amazed at his teaching. He taught with authority, and not like the teachers of the Law of Moses. 23 Suddenly a man with an evil spirit in him entered the meeting place and yelled, 24 "Jesus from Nazareth, what do you want with us? Have you come to destroy us? I know who you are! You are God's Holy One." 25 Jesus told the evil spirit, "Be quiet and come out of the man!" 26 The spirit shook him. Then it gave a loud shout and left. 27 Everyone was completely surprised and kept saying to each other, "What is this? It must be some new kind of powerful teaching! Even the evil spirits obey him." 28 News about Jesus quickly spread all over Galilee.

Luke 4 :41

Moreover, demons came out of many people, shouting, "You are the Son of God!" But he rebuked them and would not allow them to speak, because they knew he was the Messiah.

Note that Jesus was not praying for his healing, he first cast out the demon and then he was healed. It became a regular ongoing part of his ministry preaching, healing and casting out demons. Many people who need healing and deliverance do not get it because the modern church often dismisses the ministry of deliverance. The controversial issue is that many think that Christians cannot be oppressed by demons, even though they are believers, and this concept can ruffle many feathers. The devil will use any door to infiltrate our mind, body and soul so he can mess with our lives; and usually one of the first tactics is to blind us to the truth and make us easy to offend. A Christian may not be "possessed" by a demon (because the spirit of God lives within their heart), but it does not stop the demonic from interfering with a believers life.

1 John 1:9

If we confess our sins, he is faithful and just and will forgive us our sins and purify us from all unrighteousness.

Demonic deliverance starts with our awareness, when we know what we are up against we can take action. I highly recommend the book "They shall expel demons: What you need to know about demons your invisible enemy" by Derek Prince **(17)**. Take caution with doing deliverance without prayer support and the covering of a church. However, as believers our identity is in Christ and we have the power and authority to wield the Sword of God to help deliver people so do not let it scare you off. The key with deliverance is repentance, coming before God humbly brings us into alignment. Then we take authority using the name of Jesus and revoke access by expulsion (commanding the spirits to leave). Then we burn and destroy any access points or transference objects. This includes removing any offending items from your possession: books, movies, cd's, children toys, graphic t-shirts, statues or idols (buddha, eastern relics, dragons, African art), board games (Ouija board, dungeons and dragons), pornography, drugs (marijuana, cigarettes), magazines, comic books etc. Use discernment, ask the Holy Spirit to show you what is being used as a door opener so you can destroy it. Always ensure you pray the Holy Spirit fire of protection over your mind, body and soul when doing deliverance. Anoint yourself, your door and window posts with oil. Declare the line in the sand is drawn and take back authority over your home and family, and claim back the ground the devil has stolen. Don't underestimate the power of prayer where two or more are gathered. Get a team together to fast and pray in agreement with you until it breaks. Use your tools for the courts of heaven and exercise your rights. Pray without ceasing so that it becomes a lifestyle and not just a fad.

Acts 8 : 6-8

6 The crowds gave their undivided attention to Philip's message and the signs they saw him perform. 7 With loud shrieks, unclean spirits came out of many who were possessed, and many of the paralyzed and lame were healed. 8 So there was great joy in that city.

Important note: once a person is delivered it is imperative they get soul healing and commit their lives to Jesus. The scriptures show us that once the offenders are removed from a house, if they return to find it empty (no Holy Spirit) they will return in larger numbers.

Luke 11:

24 "When an impure spirit comes out of a person, it goes through arid places seeking rest and does not find it. Then it says, 'I will return to the house I left.' 25 When it arrives, it finds the house swept clean and put in order. 26 Then it goes and takes seven other spirits more wicked than itself, and they go in and live there. And the final condition of that person is worse than the first."

Now that you are aware of the situation, you are ready to take action and get your breakthrough. Here is a **seven step prayer action plan** to get the breakthrough:

1) Confess your faith in Jesus Christ and acknowledge his sacrifice on the cross on your behalf.

2) Repent of all sin, rebellion and witchcraft.

3) Claim and accept forgiveness for your sins.

4) Forgive all people who have ever hurt or offended you.

5) Renounce all contact with anything in the occult.

6) Pray the prayer of release from all curses.

7) Believe you have received forgiveness and redemption.

Remember the importance of confession. You say with your mouth what God's Word says about you. Replace negative confessions with positive one; "I wish I were dead," now becomes "I am alive in Christ".

Weapons of Warfare

For the weapons of our warfare are not carnal but mighty in God for pulling down strongholds.

2 Corinthians 10:4 (NKJV)

Did you know that worship is what the warfare is all about? God desires our worship, but the devil wants to be worshipped as well. Worship is not just what we do by raising our hands and singing praises to God in church, what we abstain from doing is also considered worship. Most believers are trying to serve God, and the enemy resorts to using deceiving methods to make them worship him instead. When we accept the things of the world it is the highest form of worship, and it opens demonic doors in the spiritual realm.

In the New Testament the word "wiles" is 'methodeia' (18) in the Greek.

It means "cunning arts, deceit, craft, trickery". This is the foundational truth of the wiles of the devil – to lie behind the scenes hiding, waiting and watching until a vulnerable moment arises so he can strike with his deceit and trickery. Then through various means or methods, all designed by the satanic kingdom, the person is attacked and deceived and he/she did not even see it coming.

2 Corinthians 2:10

We use God's mighty weapons, not worldly weapons, to knock down the strongholds of human reasoning and to destroy false arguments.

With knowledge comes power, and here are the weapons of warfare you can add to your arsenal:

(1) Armour of God

Ephesians 6:11 (KJB)

Put on the whole armour of God, that ye may be able to stand against the wiles of the devil.

We have talked about the importance of the armour of God and how it is vital in protecting us and helping us win the war (if you need a refresher go back and read it again). The crucial element is that we would never to go war without being fully protected without the proper "God Gear". The helmet of salvation protects our minds, the breastplate of righteousness protects our heart, the below of truth keeps us focus on God's truth, the shield of faith helps to repel the darts of the devil, the sword of the spirit or Word of God enables us to be on the offensive and fight back, and the gospel of peace on our feet keeps us walking on the right path. Protect yourself daily by praying the armour over yourself and your loved ones.

(2) Praise and Worship:

Psalm 150 :1-6 (NIV)

Praise the Lord.[Praise God in his sanctuary; praise him in his mighty heavens. 2 Praise him for his acts of power; praise him for his surpassing greatness. 3 Praise him with the sounding of the trumpet, praise him with the harp and lyre, 4 praise him with timbrel and dancing, praise him with the strings and pipe, 5 praise him with the clash of cymbals, praise him with resounding cymbals, 6 Let everything that has breath praise the Lord. Praise the Lord.

Another effective tactical method or weapon is praise. Praise and worship are crucial weapons of warfare that put us in a position of humility, and get us in agreement with God. Praise breaks barriers and opens the heavens over us and releases the angels to take charge of their assignment, just like the angel did in Daniel 10.

Once we have travailed, prayed and fasted, then it is time to get into alignment with God and stay in praise and worship. Celebrating before we see the manifestation of our prayers helps to keep them on their way. If we grumble and complain we hit the pause button on the conveyor belt of blessings, so praising and thanking God keeps us out of negativity. When we put on the garment of praise we put on the new man/woman. Praise creates an attitude of gratitude and places our focus on God and not our problems. You cannot be grateful and grumpy at the same time, it is a conundrum!

(3) The Word of God:

Hebrews 4:12

For the word of God is alive and active. Sharper than any double-edged sword, it penetrates even to dividing soul and spirit, joints and marrow; it judges the thoughts and attitudes of the heart.

The word of God is a mighty sword and is a powerful weapon that God has given us as both an offensive and defensive weapon. We attack the enemy by declaring God's worth as truth, and it also becomes a defense weapon against the blows or darts of the enemy. Just like Jesus did when He was tested in the wilderness, we too must declare "it is written!" and speak God's Word out loud to our circumstances.

(4) Prayer:

Ephesians 2:6

And God raised us up with Christ and seated us with him in the heavenly realms in Christ Jesus.

Prayer is another powerful weapon that we use to defeat Satan and his kingdom of darkness. It is through prayer that we tear down every stronghold of the enemy, pull down the traps and barricades he has set up against us, and we decree and declare what we want to see manifest. The Bible tells us that we are kings and priests seated in heavenly places with Christ Jesus, and God is depending on us to rule and reign over our territory. Therefore Satan is a trespasser and we have the divine right to expel him and kick him off our promised land.

(5) The Blood of Jesus:

1 John 1:7

But if we walk in the light, as he is in the light, we have fellowship with one another, and the blood of Jesus, his Son, purifies us from all sin.

The blood of Jesus is another powerful weapon of our warfare, it is God's atomic weapon for defeating the enemy. The enemy does not like the blood of Jesus because when we use it by faith by declaring it over our lives we devastate his plans. The enemy knows that the blood of Jesus defeated him at the cross so when he comes against us, we need to by faith plead the blood of Jesus over ourselves by speaking it out loud "I plead the blood of Jesus over me", and the enemy has no choice but to back off.

We must understand that not all the weapons of our warfare (19) can be used for every single battle; in some fights God will require us to worship and praise, while others will require us to defeat the enemy by fasting. What is important to remember is that you know them and how to use them effectively and allow God to guide you with the most effective strategy for each situation.

(6) The name of Jesus:

Philippians 2:5-11

5 In your relationships with one another, have the same mindset as Christ Jesus: 6 Who, being in very nature God, did not consider equality with God something to be used to his own advantage; 7 rather, he made himself nothing by taking the very nature of a servant, being made in human likeness. 8 And being found in appearance as a man, he humbled himself by becoming obedient to death- even death on a cross! 9 Therefore God exalted him to the highest place and gave him the name that is above every name, 10 that at the name of Jesus every knee should bow, in heaven and on earth and under the earth,11 and every tongue acknowledge that Jesus Christ is Lord, to the glory of God the Father.

The great news is that when Jesus humbled himself and made himself lowly by taking on the nature of a servant, he bought back the authority Adam and Even gave up in the garden of Eden. Jesus became obedient to the point of death so that God could exalt Him above every name. The name of Jesus is a powerful lighting bolt of power that cuts through all darkness, demonic forces and strongholds. Jesus was given the keys to life and death and we can rest assured that we have already won the war. It is up to us to wield our weapons with the authority that we are given through Jesus. Praise God!

Don't Give Up

But as for you, be strong and do not give up, for your work will be rewarded.

2 Corinthians 15:7

Jon Acuff wrote a book called "Finish: Give yourself the Gift of Done" (20) and he says we give up the day after perfect. You would think if you have made a big decision to lose weight, write that book, run a marathon or start a business that you would give it a bit of a try before throwing in the towel. Surprisingly most people give up on their goals on day 2; not day 21 or day 7 but on day 2. Most gyms get a boost of new sign ups in January but by February it is almost a ghost town (I say almost as there are always the full time committed and those trying to give it a good go).

Personally I am not into working out in a gym I prefer the freedom of an ice rink. When I first started skating I thought I was the bomb-diggity because I came from a classically trained ballet background. I thought because of my training that ice skating would be a breeze, but surprisingly many skating moves are counter intuitive to ballet moves. I quickly realized that if I wanted to be as grateful on the ice as Kristi Yamaguchi, I had to dig in my heels and work at it. If I gave up the first time I fell I would have never learnt anything. Instead I do the moves over and over again until they become muscle memory, I prepare to fall and expect to learn from it. The key Jon Acuff says is to cut your goal in half or double the timeline. Perfection is a liar and will first tell you that you cannot do it, but then when you decide to do it it sabotages your progress by telling you if it is not perfect so you may as well give up. Time to break up with perfect!

Jesus was tempted immediately after being anointed and Satan attacked Jesus's identity, His divinity and His calling. Jesus was tempted to give up, give in, and sell out. Can you imagine if he did? Oh my shivers down my spine! I am so grateful that Jesus had the fortitude to know who He is and not give up on His divine calling.

Luke 4 :1-13 (ESV) shows us...

1 And Jesus, full of the Holy Spirit, returned from the Jordan and was led by the Spirit in the wilderness 2 for forty days, being tempted by the devil. And he ate nothing during those days. And when they were ended, he was hungry. 3 The devil said to him, "If you are the Son of God, command this stone to become bread."4 And Jesus answered him, "It is written, 'Man shall not live by bread alone.'" 5 And the devil took him up and showed him all the kingdoms of the world in a moment of time, 6 and said to him, "To you I will give all this authority and their glory, for it has been delivered to me, and I give it to whom I will. 7 If you, then, will worship me, it will all be yours." 8 And Jesus answered him, "It is written, "'You shall worship the Lord your God, and him only shall you serve.'" 9 And he took him to Jerusalem and set him on the pinnacle of the temple and said to him, "If you are the Son of God, throw yourself down from here, 10 for it is written, "'He will command his angels concerning you, to guard you,' 11 and "'On their hands they will bear you up, lest you strike your foot against a stone.'" 12 And Jesus answered him, "It is said, 'You shall not put the Lord your God to the test.'" 13 And when the devil had ended every temptation, he departed from him until an opportune time.

If you decide to pursue your healing and work through even the most painful parts (and they will be painful), you need to give yourself grace so you can achieve your goal. Give yourself more time or cut your long list down in half, and start getting the small wins so you are motivated to keep going. Celebrate every tiny win as a big achievement because you are moving forward. Joyce Meyer says "I may not be where I want to be but thank God I am not where I used to be!" Amen sister!!!

Prayer: Praying for others

Dear Lord Jesus I come before you with a humble heart. I repent of all wrongdoing and turn from my wicked ways. I ask that you grant my petition to stand in the gap for _____ (insert name). You Lord know their situation better than I do and I ask that according to your Word in Mark 11:24 you say "I tell you, you can pray for anything, and if you believe that you've received it, it will be yours." I believe that Jesus you are the Son of God who died on the cross for our sins. I ask that you cover _____ (insert name) with the blood of Jesus and you forgive them for they know not what they do. I ask that you forgive their sins of _____ (list sins) and cleanse them of all unrighteousness. Please Lord soften their heart to receive the gospel and save them so that they come to salvation. I pray the angels encamp around them and a hedge of protection be their shield. I thank you and praise you for all that you are doing in their lives to bring them into the Kingdom and delivering them from darkness and their afflictions. In Jesus name amen!

8. Marriage Matters

Marriage Matters

A new command I give you: Love one another. As I have loved you, so you must love one another.

John 13:34

Living life, raising children, fighting demonic onslaughts, and enduring tests and trials is hard enough trying to do it alone. This is why we are called the "body" of Christ because we need each other. Where one is weak another is strong and we lift each other up. Loving each other like Christ loves the church builds unity, patience and love. For years I tried to do it alone, and would fight the hands that tried to help me out of fear, pride and rejection. But the biggest aha moment I had was when God gently showed me that I could be twice as effective by standing shoulder to shoulder with my husband.

If you are a single parent, I understand how hard it must be for you to shoulder the responsibility on your own. This is a big reason why you should surround yourself with like-minded, strong spiritual advisors and prayer warriors who can help lift you up when you are weak. Reach out to your local church and get involved so you can find heart-centered brothers and sisters who can stand in the gap with you.

Now for my marrieds, after 22 years of marriage I have some words of advice. Husbands are to love their wives, and wives are to honor their husbands. Stop trying to control your husband by creating arguments over petty little things that will cause family strife. For example, when our kids were toddlers I would get resentful when my husband went to play golf and left me to fend for the kids for the whole day. I would make a point of sulking, pouting and being demanding just because he had a day of fun and I did not. I felt sorry for myself in my martyrdom as a parent enduring pain while raising toddlers. Trying to keep a stranglehold on his activities just strained our relationship and caused more fights. Just because I was unhappy did not mean I had to make him suffer too.

Guys like their boxes, in particular their "nothing box". Mark Gungor has a hilarious video series called "A Tale of Two Brains" from his series "Laugh your way to a Better Marriage (1). The story goes that the brains of men and women are very different, especially when it comes to processing information. A woman's brain looks like a complicated ball of electrical wire. Everything is connected and driven by energy called emotion (which is why we remember everything). A man's brain is made up of boxes and he can only be in one box at a time. There is a box for money, the car, the job, the mother-in-law etc. The rule is the boxes do not touch. And then there is the nothing box, it has (you guessed it) nothing in it, and when he is in it nothing gets through!

The best marriage advice I can give you is to lower your expectations ladies. Guys cannot read our minds so that is why communication is key. He will not know how you are feeling or if you are struggling if you pout and sulk and say nothing is wrong when he asks you. Rather pull up a chair and share how you feel so that he can best support you. Guys love to fix things and save their damsels in distress so let him in to your circle. Having your husband stand with you as you pray for your situation makes you twice as effective and builds spiritual unity.

Ephesians 5:21-33

21 Submit to one another out of reverence for Christ. 22 Wives, submit yourselves to your own husbands as you do to the Lord. 23 For the husband is the head of the wife as Christ is the head of the church, his body, of which he is the Saviour. 24 Now as the church submits to Christ, so also wives should submit to their husbands in everything. 25 Husbands, love your wives, just as Christ loved the church and gave himself up for her 26 to make her holy, cleansing her by the washing with water through the word, 27 and to present her to himself as a radiant church, without stain or wrinkle or any other blemish, but holy and blameless. 28 In this same way, husbands ought to love their wives as their own bodies. He who loves his wife loves himself. 29 After all, no one ever hated their own body, but they feed and care for their body, just as Christ does the church— 30 for we are members of his body. 31 "For this reason a man will leave his father and mother and be united to his wife, and the two will become one flesh." 32 This is a profound mystery—but I am talking about Christ and the church. 33 However, each one of you also must love his wife as he loves himself, and the wife must respect her husband.

Rebellion against Authority

Remember what it says: "Today when you hear his voice, don't harden your hearts as Israel did when they rebelled.

Hebrews 3:15

Rebellion causes division. Honoring the man's rule in the home does not mean you have to be a servant. From the age of ten I was raised by a single mother who did the best that she could to raise two strong, independent women. As I grew up I was fiercely independent to a fault. I would not take help, I would not admit fault, and I certainly would not admit defeat. Sometimes being so independent has its drawbacks as it spills into rebellion.

Honoring my husbands gift of discernment took many years for me to come to peace with. I would insist on arguing with him when he could see straight through a person's agenda in an attempt to warn me of trouble. But in my stubbornness I thought I knew better, and would surge ahead without his approval, agreement or covering. When ever I stepped out in rebellion I felt convicted but I ignored those promptings and bull dozed ahead. The consequences were frustration, lack of peace, guilt (from the secrecy) and lack of success. Anything I tried without my husbands blessings would soon crumble and fall apart. Our secrets make us sick and trying to keep things from them only makes matters worse. I ended up frazzled, sick and stressed with $11,000 worth of credit card debt because I did not tell him!

God honors the marriage covenant and so must we if we are to walk in authority that Christ gives us. We have to have our hearts in the right place and our soul wounds healed if we are to be effective prayer warriors for ourselves, our children and our family. It is vital that we come into alignment with our husband as the head of our home.

Now if you have a husband who does not honor you or your marriage covenant I can fully understand why you feel justified to walk in rebellion. There is a difference in sticking with your convictions and faith if he decides to veer off into sin. But if you know that your actions are causing discord, repent quickly and ask God for forgiveness and help. When two come together in prayer and agreement, especially when you are praying for your children, there is power when it is done under the right authority of Jesus name.

2 Corinthians 2:10

If you forgive anyone, I also forgive him. And if I have forgiven anything, I have forgiven it in the presence of Christ for your sake.

Aligning as One

Submit yourselves, then, to God. Resist the devil, and he will flee from you. Draw near to God, and He will draw near to you.

James 4 : 7-10

Aligning with your husband is key to walking in victory. Those that pray together stay together. Praying for your children with your husband is very powerful as God's word says;

Matthew 18:19

Again, truly I tell you that if two of you on earth agree about anything they ask for, it will be done for them by my Father in heaven.

Regular praying, repentance, and cleaning of the home is required to maintain victory. It is never a once and done thing, you have to continually keep up your guard and protect your family and home to the enemies attacks. Never go to sleep angry and give the devil a foothold;

Ephesians 4:

26 In your anger do not sin": Do not let the sun go down while you are still angry, 27 and do not give the devil a foothold.

Pride prevents us from apologizing. Cast out that spirit of pride and walk humbly so that the enemy has no right to interfere with your marriage and your family. When in doubt repent, repent, repent!

Genesis 2:24

Therefore a man shall leave his father and his mother and hold fast to his wife, and they shall become one flesh.

Prayer: For Husbands and Wives

Dear Lord thank you for giving me the gift of my spouse. I repent of the sin of rebellion and cancel the effects of the curse of rebellion. As an act of my will I come under authority of my husband as head of our home, and under the authority of Jesus Christ. I pray Lord that you guide my spouse with divine wisdom, discernment and understanding. I thank you God that you are knitting our souls together as one flesh through our marriage covenant. I declare that no weapon formed against us will prosper and I cast down all vain imaginations and attacks in Jesus name. I plead the blood of Jesus over my spouse, our marriage and our family. Thank you Lord for breaking through spiritual barriers as we align as one. In Jesus name amen!

In conclusion, I pray for you for divine wisdom, peace and victory. Keep the faith knowing that the battle is already won!

9. Confessions and Activation Prayers

Positive Confessions: Speak out loud

Psalm 118:17

I will not die but live, and will proclaim what the LORD has done.

Habakkuk 3:19

The Sovereign LORD is my strength; he makes my feet like the feet of a deer, he enables me to tread on the heights.

Isaiah 12:2

Surely God is my salvation; I will trust and not be afraid. The LORD, the LORD himself, is my strength and my defense; he has become my salvation.

Psalm 28:7

The LORD is my strength and my shield; my heart trusts in him, and he helps me. My heart leaps for joy, and with my song I praise him.

Psalm 46:2

Therefore we will not fear, though the earth give way and the mountains fall into the heart of the sea,

Jeremiah 17:8

They will be like a tree planted by the water that sends out its roots by the stream. It does not fear when heat comes; its leaves are always green. It has no worries in a year of drought and never fails to bear fruit."

Deuteronomy 28:3

You will be blessed in the city and blessed in the country.

Psalm 118:26

Blessed is he who comes in the name of the LORD. From the house of the LORD we bless you.

Activation Prayers

Prayer: to Accept Christ

Dear Lord Jesus, I believe that you are the Son of God who died on the cross and rose again. I am a sinner please forgive me for my sins. Wash me clean with the blood of Jesus. By faith I receive the gift of salvation and eternal life. I ask you now to come live in my heart. I am ready to trust you as my Lord and Saviour. Amen

Healing Prayer: Say this prayer out loud...

By the power and authority of the matchless name of Jesus Christ I take authority over every virus, bacteria, illness in my body. I purge every toxin and poison, I curse every pathogen to die in Jesus name. Demons that have caused diseases come out now in Jesus name. By His stripes I am healed. I release health and restoration throughout my body by the dynamos resurrection power Strengthen my immune system in Jesus name. I command all diseases, inflammation, swelling to go now in Jesus name. Come out all flu, viruses and parasites in Jesus name. Spirits of fear and death I command you to go now in Jesus name. Spirits of sickness and infirmity leave now in Jesus name. Restore my body in Jesus name and make it strong to fight all attacks. All pathogenic bacteria come out now in Jesus name. Father cleanse my blood with the powerful blood of Jesus. I declare that Jesus died for me to have good health and by faith I claim perfect health in Jesus name. I repent for opening the doors to the enemy. I resist the devil and break off his hold on me in Jesus name. Thank you Lord for all you've done for me in Jesus name amen!

Deliverance Prayer: Say this prayer out loud...

Dear Lord Jesus, I believe that You are the Son of God and that you died for my sins on the cross. I believe you rose again from the dead. I repent of all my sin and rebellion and ask for your forgiveness, I submit myself completely to You and accept you as my Lord and Saviour. I ask for Your forgiveness and release from all curses I have been exposed to through my own sin, and from passed down generational sin. Release me from the consequences of my ancestors sin. By an act of my will I forgive and release all who have harmed me (both knowingly and unknowingly) just as I want God to forgive me. In particular I forgive _____ (insert names). I renounce all contact with anything satanic and occult. If I have any contact objects please show me, and I commit to destroy them. I cancel and break any claims Satan has against me. I believe you took on every curse on the cross so that I could live freely, so I ask you to release me now from every curse over my life in the might name of Jesus Christ.

References

CHAPTER 1 – MY STORY
CHAPTER 2 – ADMITTING DEFEAT
CHAPTER 3 – BARRIERS TO BLESSINGS

(1) Barriers to blessings: Martin Luther https://www.history.com/topics/martin-luther-and-the-95-theses (3/27/2018).

(2) Heartbroken: Kintsugi https://www.lifegate.com/people/lifestyle/kintsugi (1/23/2018).

Mind is the Battlefield.

(3) Soul wounds: Katie Souza "Healing the Wounded Soul" (Charisma House October 3, 2017).

(4) Soul wounds: Dunamis https://www.biblestudytools.com/lexicons/greek/nas/dunamis.html (2/5/2018).

(5) Baby steps: Download free workbook accompanying this book www.mimikacooney.com/warrior (3/27/2018).

Our Helper.

Roots.

Trauma.

(6) Trauma: Merriam-Webster dictionary "trauma" https://www.merriam-webster.com/dictionary/trauma (3/27/2018).

(7) Trauma: Traumatizo https://www.biblestudytools.com/lexicons/greek/kjv/traumatizo.html (3/27/2018).

(8) Trauma: Childhood trauma leads to lifelong chronic illness.

https://www.huffingtonpost.com/donna-jackson-nakazawa/childhood-trauma-leads-to_b_11154082.html (3/27/2018).

(9) Trauma: Researchers at Yale https://www.ncbi.nlm.nih.gov/pubmed/ 24655651 (3/27/2018).

(10) Trauma: Huffington Post http://aceresponse.org/img/uploads/file/ larkin_aces_final.pdf (3/27/2018).

(11) Trauma: https://www.ncbi.nlm.nih.gov/pubmed/19840693 (3/29/ 2018).

(12) Trauma: https://stmlearning.com/chadwick-s-child-maltreatment-vol2.html (3/29/2018).

(13) Trauma: http://www.ajpmonline.org/article/S0749-3797(98)00017-8/ fulltext (3/29/2018).

(14) Trauma: https://www.cdc.gov/media/releases/2012/ p0201_child_abuse.html(3/29/2018).

(15) Sins: https://en.wikipedia.org/wiki/Seven_deadly_sins (3/29/2018).

(16) Sins: Cardia http://biblehub.com/greek/2588.htm (3/29/2018).

(17) Sins: Koilia http://biblehub.com/str/greek/2836.htm (3/29/2018).

(18) Sins: Skotos http://biblehub.com/str/greek/4655.htm (3/29/2018).

(19) Stress: American Institute of Stress statistic 77% https://www.stress.org/daily-life/ (4/4/2018).

(20) Stress: 75-90% of doctors visits https://www.stress.org/ americas-1-health-problem/ (4/4/2018).

CHAPTER 4 – BARRIERS IN THE MIND

Negative Thoughts.

(1) Rejection: Derek Prince rejection http://www.endureinstrength.org/ pages.asp?pageid=110184 (4/2/2018).

Pride.

(2) Anger: https://www.mentalhelp.net/articles/physiology-of-anger/ (4/2/2018).

(3) Anger: https://www.betterhealth.vic.gov.au/health/healthyliving/anger-how-it-affects-people (4/2/2018).

(4) Anger: Greek word Paroxusmos http://biblehub.com/str/greek/3948.htm (4/2/2018).

(5) Anger: Paroxysm definition https://www.merriam-webster.com/dictionary/paroxysm (4/2/2018).

(6) Bitterness: Bitter pill to swallow https://dictionary.cambridge.org/us/dictionary/english/a-bitter-pill-to-swallow (4/4/2018).

(7) Bitterness: Results http://www.wholeperson-counseling.org/health/bones.html (4/4/2018).

(8) Bitterness: Reproach https://www.merriam-webster.com/dictionary/reproach (4/4/2018).

(9) Bitterness: According to Medical News Today https://www.medicalnewstoday.com/articles/285666.php (4/4/2018).

(10) Perfectionism: Symptoms https://www.psychologytoday.com/us/basics/perfectionism (4/4/2018).

(11) Perfectionism: Derek Prince Heart toward God http://www.derekprince.org/Publisher/File.aspx?id=1000021502 (4/4/2018).

Rebellion.

Reasoning.

CHAPTER 5 – BARRIERS IN MOODS

(1) Fear: The Merriam-Webster Dictionary "Fear" https://www.merriam-webster.com/dictionary/fear (3/29/2018).

(2) Fear: The online medical dictionary "fear" https://medical-dictionary.thefreedictionary.com/fear (3/29/2018).

(3) Fear: Fear not mentioned 365 times https://www1.cbn.com/soultransformation/archive/2011/10/21/fear-not.-365-days-a-year (3/29/2018).

(4) Anxiety: Anxiety and Depression Association of America "Anxiety disorders" https://adaa.org/about-adaa/press-room/facts-statistics# (3/29/2018).

(5) Anxiety: The Office of the Surgeon General study of combat soldiers http://i.a.cnn.net/cnn/2007/images/05/04/mhat.iv.report.pdf (3/29/2018).

(6) Anxiety: American Psychological Association's (APA) Journal of Personality and Social Psychology http://www.apa.org/news/press/releases/2000/12/anxiety.aspx (3/29/2018).

(7) Anxiety: World Happiness report of 2017 http://worldhappiness.report/ed/2017/ (3/31/2018).

(8) Worry: Merriam-Webster dictionary "worry" https://www.merriam-webster.com/dictionary/worry (3/31/2018).

Unforgiveness.

(9) Depression: Causes of depression are https://www.webmd.com/depression/guide/causes-depression#1 (3/31/2018).

(10) Depression: Marriam-Webster dictionary definition of depression https://www.merriam-webster.com/dictionary/depression (3/31/2018).

Self-Pity.

Guilt, Shame and Condemnation.

(11) Jealousy: Definition https://www.merriam-webster.com/dictionary/jealous (4/4/2018).

Chapter 6 – Barriers in the Mouth

Negative Words.

Judgement and Criticism.

(1) Offense: John Bevere "The Bait of Satan" (Charisma House; Revised edition May 24, 2004) (3/29/2018).

Complaining.

Religious Spirit.

CHAPTER 7 – UNLEASHING THE WARRIOR

(1) Wounded Warrior: Wonder Movie (2017) http://www.imdb.com/title/tt0451279/

(2) The Armor of God: Lisa Bevere book "Girls with Swords: How to Carry Your Cross Like a Hero". (Random House LLC, February 12, 2013).

(3) Expect resistance: Steven Pressfield "The War of Art" (Black Irish Entertainment LLC November 11, 2011).

(4) Spiritual Attacks: Skotos meaning darkness http://biblehub.com/str/greek/4655.htm (4/5/2018).

(5) Spiritual attacks: Ryan LeStrange "Overcoming Spiritual Attack: Identify and Break Eight Common Symptoms" (Charisma House 2016) (4/5/2018).

Devil is a Legalist.

(6) Courts of Heaven: Robert Henderson "Unlocking destinies in the Courts of Heaven" (Robert Henderson Ministries; Leaders Guide edition March 21, 2017).

(7) Courts of heaven: https://www.biblegateway.com/quicksearch/?quicksearch=courts&version=CEV&resultspp=25 (2/5/2018).

(8) Courts of heaven: https://people.howstuffworks.com/judicial-system.htm (2/10/2018).

(9) Courts of heaven: "Understanding the Courts of Heaven" webinar video series www.dougaddison.com (2/10/2018).

(10) Courts of heaven: https://dougaddison.com/2018/03/6-types-of-courts-in-the-courts-of-heaven (2/10/2018).

Standing in the Gap.

Repentance is the Key.

(11) Fasting & Praying: Daniel Fast http://daniel-fast.com/ (4/4/2018).

(12) Curses: Derek Prince "Blessing or Curse: You can Choose" (Chosen Books; 3rd edition September 1, 2006) (4/5/2018).

(13) Curses: Treachery https://www.merriam-webster.com/dictionary/treachery (4/5/2018).

(14) Curses: Apostasy https://www.merriam-webster.com/dictionary/apostasy (4/5/2018).

(15) Curses: Anathema http://biblehub.com/str/greek/331.htm (4/5/2018).

(16) Curses: https://www.merriam-webster.com/dictionary/anathema (4/5/2018).

(17) Deliverance: Derek Prince "They shall expel demons: What you need to know about demons your invisible enemy" (Chosen Books; Reprinted edition May 1, 1998).

(18) Weapons of warfare: Methodeia https://www.biblestudytools.com/lexicons/greek/nas/methodeia.html

(19) Weapons of warfare: http://www.biblewaymag.com/spiritual-weapons-do-you-know-the-weapons-of-our-warfare/

(20) Don't Give Up: Jon Acuff book "Finish: Give Yourself the Gift of Done" (Portfolio Group USA LLC, September 12, 2017).

CHAPTER 8 – MARRIAGE MATTERS

(1) Marriage Matters – Mark Gungor "Tale of Two Brains" DVD (Crown Entertainment) https://markgungor.com/products/the-tale-of-two-brains and https://www.youtube.com/watch?v=29JPnJSmDs0 (4/5/1028).

Rebellion against Authority.

Aligning as One.

CONFESSIONS AND ACTIVATION PRAYERS

About the Author

Mimika Cooney is a South African born Christian author, TV Host, inspirational speaker, award winning photographer, creative entrepreneur and mother of three. After experiencing severe rejection, bullying and a broken childhood; she spent years chasing accolades and addicted to approval, in the pursuit of finding worth, validation and confidence. Then God stepped in to heal her hurts, change her heart and awaken a passion for helping others seeking their purpose in life. Her book "Worrier to Warrior: A Mother's Journey from Fear to Faith" shares she personal story of overcoming fear, depression, anxiety and entrepreneurial burnout with God's help. Mimika has been an entrepreneur since she was 16 years old. She was nominated by Huffington Post as one of "50 Women Entrepreneurs to Follow in 2017". She has worked with entrepreneurs, authors, speakers and coaches with branding, marketing and video. She is passionate about empowering and equipping others to fulfill their God given purpose by sharing the message of God's love and grace with a world lost in negativity. Mimika says "Anything is truly possible when you put God first and follow His direction. Life can be tough at times by focusing on the Lord and his goodness turns everything into good. As a recovered perfectionist I'm here to tell you darling you can overcome if you break up with perfect and don't give up!"

For more info visit www.mimikacooney.com

Extra Offers

REVIEW

Your opinions are important and I truly value your feedback. As an author it is so important to get reviews so that future readers can make better decisions. Please help me by leaving your honest review on bookstores like Amazon, Barnes and Noble, Kobo, Nook, Goodreads, iTunes and other platforms. Thank you!

FREE PRAYER GUIDES

Download the accompanying free prayer guides by going to www.mimikacooney.com/warrior

JOIN OUR COMMUNITY

You're invited to become part of my community for continued prayer and support. Visit my website www.mimikacooney.com for more resources.

FREE DISCOUNT

Would you like graphics, printable prayers, eBooks, wall art, screensavers, stock images, T-shirts and Merchandise? Use this coupon to get **$5 FREE** to spend in my shop at www.shopmimika.com

COUPON CODE: **W2WBOOKOFFER**

Notes